# MAIDEN VOYAGE

# MAIDEN VOYAGE

## Five Year Anthology

## The Marquette Poets Circle

*edited by*

Richard J. Rastall

*Gordon Publications*, Gordon MI

A voyage always begins the same way. With tickets and suitcases, trunks and passports. Then there's the moment: standing on the deck of the ship, surrounded by fellow travelers, watching all that's familiar recede, shrink, vanish. Ahead, open water and possibility of something new, something miraculous. *Maiden Voyage* charts the restless seascape of the heart, its swells and troughs, coves and lagoons.

It's a journey five years in the making, and the pilgrims are as diverse as any that Chaucer dreamed up. Professors and piano teachers, philosophers and farmer's daughters. Claudia Drosen tells the story of Marjorie and the Pastor and how "humans work in mysterious ways." Regina Gort hikes through "thigh-high daisies," letting "the flat-bellied deer ticks latch." Kathleen Heideman psalms about "things built of wood" and the faith that "the frogs . . . would last forever." Each passenger on this boat has a tale to tell, a song to sing.

And, in the end, the reader learns the same lesson Odysseus learned: there is nothing sweeter than returning to home hearth where love awaits and poetry sparks and blazes.

So, pack your bags, open this book, read it the way I read it—with wonder, amazement, and admiration. Bon voyage.

---Martin Achatz, Poet Laureate of the Upper Peninsula

# Dedication

This book is dedicated to Matt Maki, the founder of the Marquette Poets Circle. Matt created the group to celebrate poetry and to guide each of us in the discovery of our inner poet. This book and the continued success of the Marquette Poets Circle are due to the solid foundation Matt built. We were enriched by his gifts as a leader and a teacher and are so grateful for his continued support.

# About the Marquette Poets Circle

The Marquette Poets Circle is open to everyone. It holds a monthly meeting usually on the first Monday of the month in the Peter White Public Library. The first hour is a workshop. The second hour is open mic. In addition, the Marquette Poets Circle celebrates the publications and readings of local authors and provide a space to share news, calls for submissions and thoughts about writing and poetry.

# TABLE OF CONTENTS

# Introduction

The purpose of this anthology is to showcase the diverse voices of the Marquette Poet Circle to a wider audience. Accordingly, each author is presented separately with a group of poems from each author. I also wanted to have each author's section complete with a biography and acknowledgments.

Poetry is art. Rather than subject the reader to my preferences, I chose to present the authors alphabetically. It is for you the reader to discover on your own which poems resonate with you.

Lake Superior has its surface and its depth. Many of these poems have a surface story and a story that runs deep. Look for all of the layers with each poem.

*Richard J. Rastall*

# Esther Margaret Ayers

Esther Margaret Ayers lives and works in Marquette, Michigan as a writer, piano teacher and accompanist. She studied at the Yeats International Summer School in Sligo, Ireland, and holds a BME in music and an MA in English, both from Northern Michigan University. In recent years she has written the librettos for two large choral/orchestral works commissioned and premiered by the Marquette Symphony Orchestra: *A Child's Requiem* by composer Thomas LaVoy (2013) and *Bagidaabii-Neyaashi* by composer Griffin Candey (2016). Her poem "White Stones" is the text of a choral piece by LaVoy which has been performed at Carnegie Hall and recorded by the Philadelphia-based professional choir The Same Stream. Other poems by Ayers have appeared in various publications, including *Passages North*. She and her husband, Dan Barrington, are the parents of five grown sons.

# In the Fall

*for Linda*

Try to remember who we are:

not single flames of maple
that lie extinguished on the ground. No,

we are the leaves of an oak,
curling inward against the cold,
the brown hands folding in prayer
who cling the longest to the tree. Nor

are we broken husks of milkweed
that relinquished their burden of summer clouds. No,

we are the roses, closing like fists
upon our seed:
burnished hard and crimson,
each with our own jagged crown.

# Morning Fog

Dog-nails on linoleum, pacing for breakfast,
the husky child scooping fistfuls of porridge,
the plate-clank and slop of the sink—

we flee the house through the back door
with steaming cups in our hands, and cross
the unmown meadow, weeds slapping our calves.

Down at McCarty's Cove we find
the morning fog in sheets across the strand
making and remaking the bed of the day.

Here then, is our life: hands round the warm mug,
sitting together on this hard bench in the fog
that gathers, lifts and gathers again;

the sun does not come. But you, old friend,
beside me you sit whistling your teakettle tune,
both freckled hands in your lap

forever peeling an orange.

## *Rugosa*

I lie flat in winter-bleached grass
on the bank above the break wall,
nose to the season: earth, my eyes level
with canes of *rugosa* darkening in their thicket;
not by bloom nor yet by green do I know them
but by these thorns, stiff with purpose,
what winter has left the rose.

# Prelude and Fugue in Early Spring

*for J.S. Bach*

*He maketh His sun to rise on the evil and the good,*
*and sendeth rain on the just and on the unjust.*

*Matthew 5:45*

## I.

In a century you could not have imagined
I sit this morning at a keyboard you never knew.
My coffee cools on the sill, outside my children play:
the girl on her tricycle, the boy with plastic dinosaurs,
while all around them spring crackles and snaps
beneath dying snowbanks. My hands, winter-stiff,
ache and balk before these cold keys—
white and black, sun on snow, the leafless oak.
Airplanes pass. I cannot pray. I open the book
to the page upon which your shadow fell, and find
the notes of black and white you left, a map
charting music, the journey you made to the glory
of God. I can only follow burdened,
dragging my life, my skein of color.

## II.

At the first note a fiddlehead fern
lifts a green scroll, calls others,
who come, curled and ancient, who pause
in new light upon their stems, trembling—
these who cannot travel but expand, rooted
in a music like sap, which must rise.
Down the block my child pedals up the hill
toward a song she can scarcely hear
above the squeak of three old wheels.
It's hard work and her legs are short;
she stops to listen, rolling backward. In the yard
my son sets snares for his beasts,
crouches inside bare bushes, sword drawn,
while lilac buds swell all around him.
The ground rumbles: from Sawyer's base thunder blooms,
a B-52 Stratofortress lumbers north, scoring the sky,
etching a staff empty of music above our heads
and vanishes over the horizon. Wind stirs, lines

6

blur, again the tricycle creaks up the hill,
the ferns still pipe their filigree of desire,
but I have lost my way—can only see
the blackest of thunder ahead, only the lightning
that bursts from the seeds of bombs.
I would leave this busy tune now—
free my son from his own trap,
push my daughter up the damned hill, hold them,
shield them with my body from the blast
of red, the barb of green—but I too am caught,
held by the fingers to my instrument,
repeating the lesson of the cliff:
*climb or die*. Outside the world has caught fire;
green jumps from stubble to stump, to fern
and bush and hill and will not stop, not even
were that lightning loosed, not even for death,
though flames spring through it and fern, girl,
son, song, my hands on the keys, all of us
groping through this fugue toward our God—

We hold our breaths
as ferns unfurl, fronds spread,
hands join here at the end,
the beginning: only us now,
rain, and the sun,
which fall and shine on the evil
and the good.

## Anything But This

Down at the bottom of February she stands
staring into the woods. Snow is falling, as it has fallen
for months. She watches it, her mind a pond of black ice,
everything sliding off. She's even forgotten why she slogged out here
to the sugar bush. Already, her tracks are disappearing
and snow begins to fill the buckets on her sled. She shivers,
slowly wakens to thoughts which have formed themselves
the way frost scribbles on windows. She'd meant to come early
but spent the morning clearing ice dams from the roof.
She thinks of taxes and numbers and she looks at the trees,
checking diameter and age: ten inches and forty years
before you could tap a maple, and then maybe eight gallons
from a tree. Forty gallons of sap to make one gallon of syrup.
She thinks of the collecting, the lifting, the hauling and the pouring;
standing there she lets all her doubts accumulate: all the years out here
raising the kids, tending the house, the garden, the woodpile,
and this business, trying to scrape by with child support, tutoring,
driving the school bus. Hell, with her education she could
have had a real job, a 401K, provided better for her old age. She could
have had a vacation, for Christ's sake, taken a cruise,
or retired at fifty, like Pauline, who paints, practices yoga
and buys pure maple syrup. Maybe Steve would've stayed
instead of running off to Boston with that woman he met
surfing the web at work. There'd been *so* much work here—
satisfaction, true, deep as the roots of these trees—
but when did they have any fun?

Gazing at the grove she wonders whether she'll even bother
tapping the trees this year. There are the odd ones who buy,
but even her own kids say the stuff is too strong. Still,
she notes how the light has grown: the forest is heavy with it;
from below the snow has begun its long surrender
and each warming tree rises inside a halo of thaw.
She draws off a mitten, holds up one palm: flakes,
feathered and grey, float down and lie melting on her hand.
It comes to her that today is Ash Wednesday. So, here it is— Lent.
Something like prayer, knotted within her, roots and gropes,
but she jams her hands back in the chaps, shucks off the snow
muttering, *well I can sure as hell give this up.* Turning back,
she jerks the sled around. That's when she sees it—
the sugar house— shuttered and sleeping at the edge of the clearing,
with its clean bleached logs and louvered cupola,

the cordwood stacked and ready since the fall:
one cord for every twenty-five gallons.

She knows there's plenty of kindling just inside the door,
imagines lighting the tinder: hears the snap and hiss,
the slosh of each bucket of sap into the wide pan
and she remembers what it's like to squat and wait
and skim the foam and debris that come up when it boils;
to feed the flame, stick by stick, under the liquid
that thickens and darkens with each turn of the baffle,
and what it's finally  like to taste
the amber sweetness dripping into the glass…

at last she turns again to the trees;
pushing on, she knows
she can give up anything—

anything but this.

# Milton J. Bates

Milton J. Bates is the author of nonfiction books about the poet Wallace Stevens, the Vietnam War, and the Bark River valley in Wisconsin. A former Guggenheim Fellow, he was a Fulbright lecturer in American literature at Beijing Foreign Studies University and the Universidad Complutense de Madrid. Five Oaks Press published his chapbook *Always on Fire* in 2016 and nominated one of the poems for a Pushcart Prize.

## Supposing the House Is on Fire

It's a game we play. *Suppose the house is
on fire*, we say. *What would you try to save?*
Our children aren't for saving anymore.
They've grown up and moved to houses of their own.
No pets either, to complicate the choice.

You open with the jeans you'd grab because
you've never had a pair that fit so well.
I counter with my lucky fishing rod.
We're just warming up, passing the time
until one of us plays the winning card,
the same one every game. We'd rescue our
photos first, low-crawling through smoky rooms,
dodging the falling embers and sparking wires
because we can't bear to lose the story
pictures tell, the proof we've walked this earth.

We tried a retrospective once, gorging
nightly on prints and slides, devouring
digital images. We remarked how young
we looked, how peculiar our clothes,
how we really must return to destination
x or y. The surfeit left us still unsatisfied.

*What's missing from the record?* we asked
ourselves, and had to answer, *almost everything*.
It's a game we play, the picture-taking too.
Who'd ever guess that we sipped coffee
as the sun came up, spent most days working,
touched each other in the dark? Pictures
don't lie. But they keep secrets, including
this one: the house is always on fire.

(This poem first appeared in the summer/fall 2015 issue of *Dunes Review*.)

## The Darkroom

When he needed to see things clearly,
he retreated to a walled-off corner
of the basement, switched on a red light,

and poured potions from brown bottles into trays.
Then he fed a filmstrip into the enlarger
and twisted the lens until his world snapped

into focus. It wasn't as he remembered
it, not yet, but the photo paper's
silver salts would make it right again,

turn black to white and white to black. He threw
an image onto the light-shy surface,
counted down, and eased it into a tray.

A picture bloomed in the seiche-like sloshing
of developer. He bathed it in fresh water,
locked it in with fixer, and rinsed it off.

Under white light the likeness seemed true
enough, but not as true as one he'd glimpsed
before the grays turned black. He'd heard

of images like that, shimmering above
the polar ice or desert sand. Shapes that weren't
quite there. Things seen once, seen truly,

never seen again. He hung the print
to dry and climbed the stairs to daylight,
climbed slowly toward that other darkness.


(This poem first appeared in the spring 2016 issue of *The Southern Review*.)

## Chinese Folk Song Performed
## on Oldest Playable Flute

It was all about air, how it passes
over mortal things. When the bone was
still fleshed and fledged, it made a slight
creaking sound as the great bird flew
over mountains. It lay mute and folded
as the bird stilt-walked the marshes
or clamored with the other red-crowns,
their slender bills pointing skyward
like reeds along the Yellow River.

The bone survived the bird. A man
of Jiahu drilled seven holes for air to come
and go as his lips and fingers pleased.
Even then the bone sang its own song,
an elegy for cranes and men, as though
it could hear the coming silence, foresee
the nine millennia of midnight.

At last a hand reached out of light
to lift the bone, clay-clotted, from its grave.
Soon it felt lips again, and fingers,
teasing air into tendrils of melody.
It half-learned and half-remembered
how Little Cabbage missed her mother,
especially in the spring, when the air
was sweet with peach and almond blossoms.

(This poem first appeared in *Encore: Prize Poems 2014*, a publication of the National Federation of State Poetry Societies.)

## Bereft, He Chooses a Grave Marker

Stone
would not do, granite or marble polished
to give back a face he knew too well,
etched with grief. Fine-grained as glass
or steel, impervious, it would tell
his fingertips too much, too soon,
about the permanence of loss.

Wood
it would have to be, red oak from a tree
like those that framed her garden. It would
weather like their marriage. It would need
attention. He'd massage it weekly
with fragrant oil, feeling in its grain
the familiar texture of her skin.

Earth
would claim him too, so he'd have another
ready for himself. With no one
to anoint them the slabs would check
and warp, turn gray and crumble
into dust. This he could foresee.
This was how it had to be.


(This poem first appeared in the summer/fall 2015 issue of *Dunes Review*.)

## Superior Ice-Out

Living by the lake, we don't trust returning
birds to tell us winter's over. We watch
the ice and listen. For weeks we've heard
it whoop and detonate offshore, seen
the plates it's piled into windrows. More
docile now, it fractures quietly along
its fault lines. Water shows like ink between
snow-dusted geometric panels—squares,
rectangles, diamonds, trapezoids.
Then a wind disturbs the slabs, smudging
the neatly ruled lines. We look away,
distracted for a moment by less
momentous goings-on, then look back
to find the landscape rearranged. The sheets
are gone, replaced by what? Dragon scales?
Acres of honeycomb? Salt craters from
a dried-up sea? Freighter pilots call it
pancake ice, making of our flesh-numbing lake
a flesh-searing griddle. The cakes crunch
and jostle, fizz and tinkle, their edges
growing rounder as they socialize.

That's our cue to creep from winter houses,
to blink in the mid-March sun like hostages
released. We walk our dogs and check our
mailboxes, bumping into neighbors
who look familiar, remembered from
another time and place. Our voices sound
unnatural when we stop to talk, a bit
too loud, as though we're trying to be heard
above the slosh and sizzle of the ice.

(This poem first appeared in *Always on Fire* [Newburgh, NY: Five Oaks Press,
    2016].)

# A. Lynn Blumer

A. Lynn Blumer has lived in Michigan's Upper Peninsula for nine years. She's been writing books since she knew how to fold paper and staple it together, but became an author with the self-published anthology *N: Poems and Short Stories.* After which she started her business *Pyre Publishing* with help from fellow writer *Troy Graham.* *Pyre* has since published *N: Volume Two* and is now working towards *N: Volume Three* as well as running the *ez.P.zine.*

Blumer has also been published with *Horror Sleaze Trash* in their *HST: Quarterly,* her work can be found in all three volumes of *N,* and her personal collection of poems, *Blur Every Line,* will be released in 2018.

She also really likes her dog, hiking, and has a fascination with reptiles

# Just Human

There is something about the way
The wind beats against the trees
That eats at the very barrier within me
&I am reminded again
That I am just human.

I am just Man reaching
For a higher understanding,
As well as
A higher standard of living,
But when, pray tell,
Did all the material bullshit
Get in the way?

When did self-awareness
Become self-consciousness?
When did my will to survive
Become my urge to spend more?

I am just Man
&I must have the
Latest fashion to attract
A mate &intimidate
The competition.
I must exercise
&Listen to my dietitian
Since everything in this world
Is just given to me.

I am just Human
&My instincts have been
Turned against me.
I live amongst buildings—
Artificial mountains
Detained by their streets,
&The street ruled
By the grid in which
Human existence is now
So neatly contained.

You can't see the Forest
For the Bricks—
The wandering Trail
For the Concrete—
The Human
For the Crowd.

No wonder we've
Lost sight so easily.

We've lost sight of
How simple the task
Really is—
Hunt, Gather, Live.
It's all been overly simplified
In a complicated way.
Now we're left
just looking at each other.

What's worse
Is when one's sight
Is only as far as
A cell phone's light—
When one's reach
Is only as far as
A computer screen.

Somedays, I could smash it all
With my bare hands.
This hand held devise
Is trying to put my life
In a rectangle
&The wild Animal
Doesn't. Quite. Like. It.

I tease myself with the thought
Of how easy it would be
To just fold the thing in half,
Yet, I can't.
It feels like my only
Life line now
&I am horrified
That this is how my
Life lies now.

I am just Human
&That is all
I want to be.

I want to listen to the wind
Beat against the trees
&Smell the dirt beneath me feet.
I want to earn my food
Directly with my wit
Beside this body—
This capable, nature-made
Piece of work
So many take for granted.

So many never see
The utility Evolution
Has finely whittled
To maintain motion.

So many stand in
Stagnant waters while
Bacteria whittles away
For the day it will take
Them out at their feet.

So many will fall….

I am just Human
&I listen when this Earth speaks.
Man screams
&The trees sing sonnets
Of honest Green.

"I am,
&will be,
Just on Man."

But,
I am just Human
&That is all
I want to be.

## Just on Man

Watch it all
Come
Crum-
bling
Down.

The
Fall.

Y'all though it
Wouldn't happen.
Consume all you want
&The Hammer
Would never drop.

No…
Not on you.
But you see,
It's *on you.*

My Human
Turned
To Man who
Stands alone.

I couldn't sing sonnets
Loud enough
To have you back
In my Bosom,
So Sirens rise
In the night
While you dash
Yourselves against
Concrete!
The hospitals
Can't hold ya,
&this mother
Has let go.

You'll be on
Your own when
Your lights
Go out.

We could've all
Had each other, but
I'll see you sleep
In the briny, bitter deep.
Putrefied amongst plankton.

Density, after all,
Is what you
Insisted on….

Every life
You found precious
*I had to feed.*
The Fuel &the Toil
You took, I'll take back
*more densely*
6 billion bodies
Worth of bones
How *tense* each
Compression
*Makes thee.*

The Toil
It took.
I assure
You…
I'll be
Taking
That Oil
Back.

# Maria

Maria, Maria,
Wouldn't want
To be ya.

So beautiful
They all could
Eat ya…

Maria, Maria…

You tap a counter top
A marble so cold
Worth its weight in gold
The sound—it sounds the same
No matter how many lines
& curves it can bounce over.

It's echo.
It's void.
It's there.
Where is it?

Maria, Maria…

They all wanted
A piece of ya.
They rummaged—
They're rubbish.

Maria, Maria…

There ain't a lot-a
To ya, but
There's a lot
Of to-ya
To sort through.

You are a rat in a pot
Of boiling water with
Its stomach popped.

You are a sink rag.
You are a floor rag.
Your stomach is tight.
Maria, Maria...

They all thought
They could fix ya
When all ya could do
Was run.

They caught ya
& put ya down soft
On comforters.
They built up their walls
Strong—around ya
They all longed
& left behind
All their big tools
That were meant for you.

Maria, Maria...
Ya just wanted to fill it.

Maria, Maria...
Its always coming
Back to ya.

Maria, Maria...
MARIA, MARIA...
MARIA! MARIA!

So loud
You could smash it
With your biggest
Fucking hammer!

MARIA!

MARIA!

MARIA!

SHATTER—you did just that.

Maria, Maria...

So beautiful
None of them
Could see ya.

Maria, Maria...
Wouldn't want
To be ya.

## The Dead River

It's a half moon,
just enough to move through
this sheltered trail—a meander
to the cold concrete bridge,
a pass where you now sit.

It's trauma to depart you
&here one piece is found on
a distant train you can relate with its keen,
inanimate scream coming through the trees.

Parallel rails draw out the sound so
unlike any human embrace or emotions like iron never knew
how to hold even a simple conversation you can relate with that,
at least there is contact.

Though for the rest,
there is none—not for the undead—
it's a visceral kind of numb that keeps you up
&away to where the dead run,
wallowing over bedrocks.

So here you sit,
&listen to the long way the gone speak
leaking their stream of ceaseless dark
you could at any thought get caught in.

But remember,
you're at about a half moon
—basking back,
you can feel it waxing
with animate coos.

24

## Bloody on The Floor

"What is that?"
The guests ponder
& I couldn't utter an answer.
My dog had thrown up
A white lump presented
For a living room of
People to gawk at.
As the third one hit the floor,
I saw the string flop mid-wriggle
Aside the soggy glob in question.

That night was the first time.
It was a total of five
Gash swollen sums with
Kind of chewed dog food
& internal fluid pooling
As I turned white.

Then it was one,
Two,
Sometimes
Three.
You hacked
Me up like
This act
Somehow
Made us one.

Anything to be closer, right baby?

Now the moon is
Almost full again
&I know what's
Said once they have
A taste for blood.

I'm not bloody yet,
But I'm clearing out a space
Under the sink for the bin,
Saying:

"I can't afford a vet. I can't afford a vet."

# Lynn Domina

Lynn Domina is the author of two collections of poetry, *Corporal Works* and *Framed in Silence*, and the editor of a collection of essays, *Poets on the Psalms*. Her recent work appears in *The Portland Review*, *Pembroke*, *New Letters*, The *Gettysburg Review, Poetry Daily*, and many other periodicals. She currently serves as Head of the English Department at Northern Michigan University and lives in Marquette.

## Bear

At first I saw slumped shadow,
a dark just darker than autumn darkness.
Then I distinguished sloped shoulder, snout,
bulky hind leg. I saw her head tilt.
I saw the garbage cans
where she'd dragged them. She sat
a while longer, eating, not eating, as I watched
from our lightless kitchen. Time shifted
as when a river
begins to flood. I watched her
amble toward a brake of oak saplings.
I saw her merge into night until the space
that had held her held
only night, a globe of darkness
I wished to enter
but could only dispel.


(This poem first appeared in *Nimrod*.)

# Whispered

--for Elizabeth Oakes

Mercy is a woman I'd like
to offer a cup of coffee. I'd like to see
her hands fold around a brimming mug as she remembered
skating across a broad pond, the ice
thick, clouded, blue enough to suggest
water rippled beneath her. I'd like to behold Mercy
content with memory, consoled by thin light
stippling her bare wrist. I could turn
and whisper her name. *Mercy*, I could say,
and she would lift her eyes, her gaze
resting on my face as I felt
my body lighten, the word
eased from my lips, *Mercy, Mercy.*


(This poem first appeared in *Ruminate*.)

# The Road to Happiness

*a streak of light visible upon a breeze-*
*wrinkled surface of water is called*
*"The Road to Happiness"*
                    *Monte Reel*

Cresting the hill west of Seymour,
past shiny signs proposing chicken sandwiches,
breakfast all day, larger coffee, biscuits,
new flavors, and past two Chinese
buffets rumored to be closing
forever, and past the auto parts store,
insurance agency, and cheap hair salon
where young women wax
my eyebrows, and always past a snowplow
spitting sand and the car wash that opens
only after temperatures rise
above twenty, and past the school bus
carrying cheerleaders to the township
and the pick-up stacked with storm windows,

I look up to see, again, the lake
stretching, I know, to another country,
and I take its blue measure,
and I take in its wind-brushed
surface, its narrow breakwater crusted
with ice, clouds dropping to a near horizon, and I know
I don't want to live forever,
but I want to live
here forever.

(This poem first appeared as a broadside published by *Winter Cabin Press*.)

## Every Bulbous Cell

If I could, I would
bless the elephant
whose footprint spreads
wider than both my hands
resting in its mud cast;
I would bless her trunk
looping behind her head,
river water sprayed
across her dusty back, her delight
filling blustery exhalations. I would bless

groundhogs, the mother, two juveniles
scurrying to their den. I would bless
their waddle, their stunted legs, their prints
preserved in summer mud. Watching
them chew new blades, preferring bluegrass
seedlings to clover flowers or dandelions,
I would bless excitable hunger.

And I would bless the blue whale,
her skeleton, its string of vertebrae
curving toward her spread tail.
I would bless baleen, algae, blue oxygen
misting from her blowholes—even the muck
her flesh settles into, her buoyancy
gone, this life relinquished.

Oh who am I
to bless these creatures
who require no blessing.
And yet I do. I extend

my blessing to the thick rush
of muddy floodwater, the clutch
of maples wavering through sludgy whorls.
I bless catfish, crayfish, stunned tadpoles,
exhausted earthworms. I bless
each species of bacteria
scuttling through my gut,
all their hairy filaments, every bulbous cell.

(This poem first appeared in *Friends Journal*.)

# Peregrination

In my house—I respond
to the student who asks why
can't I just say walk?—
we say we're going to perambulate
the dog because the dog
understands the word walk and barks himself
into a frenzy if ever he hears
walk; he even knows
w-a-l-k, so we've brainstormed
synonyms, for example mosey which clarifies his style
now that he's seven and August heat
discourages the hip-hop skitter
and pounce he practiced his first fall,
attacking each red leaf
flitting across the sidewalk as if it were
some invasive rodent. And walk insufficiently
suggests his gait—he swings
and swaggers; freshly bathed,
he sashays across our one-lane bridge,
amusing drivers patient enough to watch
his dainty strut as he sniffs
clumps of fur stuck in tar,
crushed soda cans, milkweed
thrusting itself through gravel. He lunges
up the dark meandering root-snarled path
because after blizzards he's permitted
to leap drift to drift, cooling his pink belly
as I straggle and stumble, sweating through wool and down,
pausing to identify tracks: deer, skunk, turkey, dog.
Warm evenings, he backs his haunches
into stinkweed, prowls soggy ditches, shambles
through alfalfa and fresh-cut hay.
Squirrels scuttle from ash to oak, safely
beyond his curiosity or the interest
of my student who's trudging now
in his mind up the impossibly
steep steps of this assignment,
schlepping instructions from table to carrel to desk,
limping, staggering under their yoke
while I saunter home, oblivious, indifferent,
because it's easy for me, he's certain,
this jaunt, this stroll, this ramble.          (This poem first appeared in *Zone 3*.)

31

# Jo Doran

Jo Doran (1950-2015). Jo was born and raised in Michigan's Upper Peninsula and for the last several years of her life lived in Marquette, where the Marquette Poets Circle was very important to her. Her poetry, articles and stories appeared in many journals and magazines, and she was an avid blogger on language and writing pedagogy, knitting, and grief. Jo was intimately acquainted with grief, and the last months of her life were devoted to writing a book on grief, which her illness prevented her from completing. Her poems for this anthology were selected to give voice to her desire to write grief large.

# LIERNES

*Cathedral Church of the Blessed Virgin Mary, Hereford, England*


The ceiling's spine, the meeting place
where oblique ribs join single cusps of leaves:
three in each rise out of the muscle of stone.

The skin of the ceiling, damask, patterned
symmetry is flushed with verdure.

These are ridge ribs, transverse, intersected
beauty as well as strength, curved
crosswise  at right angles to the body's backbone.

———————————————————————


If we could see past our blood, this is how we would look:
our chest risen, full of the breath of the gods, our breadth
matched against infinity, our cavity engraved, etched with the
outline of our lives: betrayal, abandonment, and loss.

———————————————————————


This is an image of you, my son, a treasury adorned
from within, adored from a great distance: a Damascene inlaid
with an extravagance of nerve, an impression remembered.

An echo entombed within the smallness of a grave,
within the seriousness of shadow upon shadow.

Yet even this mighty cathedral could not contain you, enshroud
your silhouette: it must reside in the angled darkness
of my own reproach, drawn along the longitude of my ribs.

# A Storm Quietly Brewing

Wilson's old maple got cut in two last night,
sliced straight through by a sheet of white fire.
It was in that time right before a storm when an all
too quiet orangeness in the sky causes people to stop
half way, as Old Mr. Potter did just then,

one hand on the next tomato, head cocked to one side

like he was listening for the weekly tornado siren check
that comes at Tuesday, noon. The one time
of the week the south-side scatters its young. Strange
how we expect something so different from what we get,

because we're bent in another direction. Because

our memory serves us, or doesn't. And looking at the sky
blue of Mr. Potter's shirt I thought how no one
in our family has ever seen him any way but old,
tried to picture him smooth, with an unhampered fire, as I have

my father, seeing him in a cream colored photograph: one knee

bent with his toe resolute to the ground, arms
crossed over his chest as though determined to force
a peace, the kind that comes right before a storm.
Today, Jimmy Paquette rode down the street

parting the silence, his bicycle wheels slapping

with red and white Diamond Playing Cards
clothes-pinned to his chipped, brown spokes. A plaid
flannel shirt too large on his ten-year old frame.
And I watched the rhythmic swing of his arm throwing

the evening paper, Jimmy never looking up,

up as my cousin did after a wind storm:
standing under the cranky burr oak at the narrow
end of Betsie Creek. He stood there staring
so hard at that tree that he never saw the twig that hit

his eyeball. He told me later that it didn't even hurt,

how he never let his mother know that he couldn't see
anything out of that eye for three months.
And I wondered how he felt; if losing part of his sight
made time stand still, like photographs do,

like the one of my father: tan trench coat and carefully

creased fedora, a Bogart lean on the garage
behind his father's pharmacy; a split
second of looking to a future: college sweetheart,
drugstore and soda shop, Harley with a side car,

a marriage of two whiskey drinking families bent

on a lean into the future, which kids never seem
to worry about. And when I asked my cousin if he wasn't
afraid that his eye would never be any good he told me
he just figured that it would work out. Like my father's

life did. But not as he imagined. Inheriting the store
but losing three wives to the grave before he buried his memory.

Finally giving up every sense of expectancy. Or perhaps
changing it, which we all have to do when the sky splits open.

## Over Ripe

It is said that cherries cleanse the blood,
rinse the circling stream of determined
limitations that whisper themselves

back, crowding the narrow arteries
and veins with desire, longing, lust,
satisfactions that window themselves

deep in the eyes: clear and clean.

And raspberries, delicate, easily destroyed,
also, touch the blood, offer
a scent of rose that escapes when blue

turns red – a pin prick, a wrist slash, releasing
the astonished messenger desperate for air;
with cherries, smooth, firm covering

on the bone of seed, combine their sudden
presence through this sleepless flow,
channel their distant escape from the body

of a lover, the vessel of a heart.

## When I Return to Prague After My Death

Still – I will be –

    the single blade of sun across your door,

        the old man waving dusty rags from the high

    eyelid of a window, the slow curve of curb


    and stone that pauses in the shade of quarrels, the abandoned

        bark of a whipped dog. I will be

    the embroidered breath of linden trees, suffocating


    the stars, breathing through the bones of night

        until summer is undone. I will be

    this. . . empty. . . of questions, the absent mind


    of your father as he mumbles in the night,

        the soft furrow of skin on the nape of the girl

    in church, who listens, and hears, angels. I


    will be as undone as the length of quiet

        in your sleep, your trouble and your tongue,

    your sullen tolerance for beauty not your own


    that glistens in the memory of death.

(This poem was previously published in *Chariton Review* and is reprinted here with permission.)

# Claudia Drosen

Musician and poet Claudia Drosen is a native of Brooklyn, New York, who left behind city life and resides with her family in Marquette, Michigan, on the Upper Peninsula's South shore of Lake Superior. Claudia is principal flutist in the Marquette Symphony Orchestra, and an Adjunct faculty member in the Music Department of Northern Michigan University. She has an M.A. in Creative Writing from Northern Michigan University, where she was a preliminary poetry reader for *Passages North* and a B.F.A. in Flute Performance from the University of Wisconsin-Milwaukee. Her poetry has appeared in *The Poetry Society of Michigan's Peninsula Poets, Lit UP, The Driftwood Review, Lips, Water Music: The Great Lakes State Poetry Anthology.* She is also a member of the band *Radio On*, a group comprised of both classical and rock musicians and singers, who, by way of original musical compositions and poetry, experiments with sound through imaginary landscapes. Claudia is also a serious proponent of frequent and unbridled laughter.

# Name

A name on a page egotistically
highlights itself when it is
*that* name, *his* name, *her* name,
the name of the just met and newly cared about,
a name that one moment before
was just as plain as the word plain.
A name you knew, a name
shared by trillions, but it could be
screamed before and still missed.

It could be mundane, matter-of-fact,
like cheese or shoes, something lost in the
shuffle, overlooked, unnoticed.

Not now. Now it is newborn, almost
makes you blush when you hear it.
It could be an unassuming Sally or Ned,
but it feels lascivious when you say it,
like motherfucker, like masturbate,
so nasty, just delicious.

Now it is not just a name, it is new music,
such a good idea, as rare as a glimpse at truth,
the first burst of a chocolate on your tongue.
This name. *His* name. *Her* name.

## What a Dove Does

As dawn crowns,
the soft, modal chant
of a mourning
dove
fills
dead
air.

At first phrase, his aural
lament strictly
calibrates
to new sun,
exiting moon-
tronomes,

but in the blink
of an avian eye,
he relaxes his coo,
and, using musical license
as his guide,
makes
a
ritard...

at the end of
each    repeti-
tion.

The same.

Each.

Time.

Breaking your
heart.

Each.

Time.

# The Silent Language of a Working Marriage

In the sun-striped living room he sheds his shirt.
Not for sex. For utility. After Saturday errands at Target—
coffee filters, Q-Tips, kitty litter, a clown-shaped birthday card
shouting *You're Four!,* Bounce sheets, flashlight batteries,
they arrive back at their drive, close their car doors in

almost unison, get looks, licks from the bored cat,
the jazzed up dog, and settle in to regroup before lunch.
In the sweet quiet, they can hear the dog gazelle
back onto the couch, twirl three times, and
sigh as she puts her foot brakes on.

Oh, sorry. I left her husband bare-chested.
He siphons 40 gallons of old water out of the aquarium,
squeaks off the algae from the glass, carries green bucket
after green bucket, Sorcerer's Apprentice-style to the
bathtub, building a new waterbed for the fish.

Jockeying back and forth down the narrow hall, they cross paths,
his wife toting a laundry bin of folded towels. They step aside
awkwardly, almost breaking out in laughter, as if to say
"No, *you* go." "No, please, I'll wait. *You.*"
He tires, kicks the bucket with one knee, water surging

onto the carpet. He shakes his head as he silently swears to himself.
She goes to the nearby dining room table to sort through snail
mail, decide if there's anything besides bills that needs to be kept.
Nothing. Zipping open credit card offers wearing 0% interest-'til-
the-end-of-time ads on their envelopes, coupons for sugar-laden

drinks, flyers from starched-shirted, backward-thinking local politicians,
she grimaces at all the wasted paper. They don't talk out loud.
They figure they'll do that at lunch. But they *are* talking.
The air vibrates with a comfortable,
tacet dialogue that fills  the house like humidity fills the throne room.

After the fish are free to explore their see-through digs,
he hangs the new shower curtain without her prodding.
She hears him unhook the old and install the new,
both cascading over the tub like vinyl waterfalls.
They are not surprised when they have little to discuss at lunch.

# After the Sermon

So, at 10 minutes past in the
chilly church basement
on potluck Sunday
(grey meatloaf,
greyer potatoes,
three-bean salad),
Pastor Whitman's unattached
family friend and bookkeeper,
taller-than-is-comfortable-for-a-woman
Marjorie, who has been
conspicuously absent from services
since who-knows-when,

storms into the smooth-floored Methodist
mess hall, fiddles uneasily with her
tortoiseshell headcomb,
(the one etched with a red-throated loon
        that her niece really likes),
throws herself to her knees,
tries to hold back full-bodied sobs.

Just about all munching and
mumbled pleasantries
screech to a halt, as Marjorie
admits to the congregated that
Hell is where she belongs, for she has been
loving Pastor Whitman in a
man-inside-woman sort of way for the last
eighteen months, and even as she confesses,
she daydreams his jittery hands fumbling
inside her blouse, and places southward.

Marjorie rubs her mascara-ringed eyes,
brings news that she is carrying his fetal
parishioner, that she wants to come clean.
Most park their forks on the long tables and
gasp—Pastor W. almost chokes on his
Snickerdoodle as his eyes avoid his
wife's face, probably white as a
Minnesota winter by now,

but Mrs. Morgan, who works at Jo-Ann Fabrics,
and her friend Betty Hanes from
Thursday night knitting circle, continue to
sip their coffee. These two obedient
pew-fillers of the flock, have known since
they laid narrow-slitted eyes on Marjorie
two years ago, that she was a
Homewrecker,

that their innocent Pastor, not capable of
instigating wrongdoing, would
fall prey to her wiles, oh yes. But they still
brim with faith that their Lord is
benevolent, fair, will open up His
forgiving heart to this duet of
sinners, and somehow understand that
humans work in mysterious ways


## Breakfast with Grandma

It's done. Overcooked to perfection.
A heavenly, burbly mush that
plops at us like it's sassing off as
Grandma Z removes the pot lid.

She doles it into bowls and dresses it with
molasses-y chunks of dark brown sugar
that sit on the surface for a second or two,
then succumb to the waves of grain,
melting into smooth brown bumps,
like the mole on her left cheek,
right above her laugh line.

# Amber Edmondson

Amber Edmondson is a poet and book artist living in the U.P. on a
decommissioned Air Force base that is probably super haunted. She is
the author of two chapbooks, *Darling Girl* (dancing girl press 2016)
and *Lost Birds of the Iron Range* (Porkbelly Press 2017). She tries to
be a good friend to her cats.

## Mating Ritual

Is it a courtship
if I tell you
I carry a pocket knife?

If I show you
my collection
of railroad spikes,
rusted bolts,
crumbled bricks?
Iron and sandstone,
the earth pulled up.

If I carry a box
but can't tell you
what's inside,
is that a ghost story
or a love song?

Love carves the deer's antler
to make a blade handle.
Wraps it in leather.
Sews it with sinew.

Love carries a broken compass
but insists it points north.

Insists that everywhere
is north. Tell me
these clouds look like snow.


(This poem first appeared in *Persephone's Daughters* (Issue 2).)

## What the Owl Loves

I'm trying to love you
like the owl loves
the vole's bones.
The stuff you spit out,
that won't dissolve
into your body,
your blood stream, the stuff
that stays separate,
that holds its shape.

I'm trying.
There's that.

You are cleaving chips
from stone, flinting
the edges. You
are gathering water.

I'm asking how I might love you,
calcium and marrow, how
I might love you, small mammal
skittering under
leaf litter, snow pack.
I'm asking
the shed and matted fur,
hibernation den.

We will bury this someday.
Dig a hole for these bones.
Split the salmon
on these river stones;
use our teeth to pull out
what we intend
to keep. Let
the current take
the rest.


(This poem first appeared in *MockingHeart Review* (Issue 1).)

## Slag

Here,
we gravel
the roads
purple, green,
and pink,
each one
paved with
what they've hauled
from the ground.

Here,
they say,
our bones
are composite
carbon,
and when
we strike
them together,
they are headlamp
birdsong.

You and I
sow seedlings
in mine shafts.

We work
with what
we've got.


(This poem first appeared in *Midwestern Gothic* (Issue 10).)

# Winter, Superior

You could heal yourself
at the palm of the lake
all winter long.

It inflates
and deflates
like a living lung
on the shore,
its breath harnessed,
black and deep.

There are deer tracks
on snow-covered ice,
a weaving path
from the black cliffs
and down to the place
where the ice slopes
at the edge and
into the water.

You could match
the quiet of the doe
who came before dawn
to drink, to trust
the thickness of ice,
the graceful sound
of shattering.

## Locomotive Heart

The dead sparrow is still
this tiny fever of feathers
in your palm, and you wonder
what it would take to fashion a heart
from copper and steam,
a hundred whistling valves and
gears and levers and finally

the fragile, liquid twitch
of black eyes. You wonder what
it would take, the pumping and
the heaving, the breathing. You wonder
what it would take. It would take
a man in love with machines.
It would take a man in love.

(This poem previously appeared in *Border Crossing* (Fall 2013 issue) and *Darling Girl* (dancing girl press).)

# Regina Gort

Regina Gort began scribbling poetry in notebooks at a young age - influenced
by West Texas deserts and summers with her grandparents on Lake Superior. At
12, the Upper Peninsula pines became home but her travels to the Dominican
Republic and her father's homeland, Puerto Rico, imparted wisdom, wonder and
wanderlust. A mother to three daughters, she's a classically trained chef who collects
and forages food while hammering ideas into poems as deep as Lake Superior.
Regina prefers thimbleberries to huckleberries but will eat either by the handfuls,
fresh or jammed atop her morning toast.

Tim and Regina Gort are poets who write collaboratively and individually. Their first
collection of *poetry, The Year of the White Tiger,* is a result of their hard work to
sustain and overcome, and is a true reflection of their love for living poetry, their
children and one another.

# Without thimbleberries

When two drips from a tablespoon dangled
sideways forge together, before it drops
into the boiling seed-full solution,
the jam is ready.

How does my blood fall when pricked by memory's pin?

Certainly we can't be one
in a glass jar, lidded under pressure
and heat. We'd break
our vessel. Stir. Stir. Scrape
the sides to keep from sticking.

This summer rain didn't come in time.

We didn't pick berries
near the concrete bridge anchors.

We didn't use grandma's silver
pot and spoon. Without scouting walks
down the two-track to the sandy beach,
you gave me no beach glass.

No one scooped
from the bottom
to keep from burning.

## Picking Ticks

Over the Escanaba River lowlands
and down the electric pole line buzz halo,
I brush against long grasses,
let the flat-bellied deer ticks latch.

They crawl up my red boots, torn jeans and scurry
beneath long shirt sleeves. Infested, I limp
toward a prehistoric crane's call.

Thigh-high daisies and cattail barriers build
but her sandpaper voice continues. I don't find her
on the reed basket nest she protects.

A multitude of ticks, thin and brown,
inch closer to my now blood-soaked pant leg.
My left leg incision weeps in strain.

I stop.

A yellow lighter in my flannel pocket.

Flick. Flick. Fire.

I set flame to a tick, closest to my wound.

It drops.

I stop.

If only I'd lit that black-ridged spot, raised and angry,
melanoma scraped out by a surgeon.

Now, a tick on my neck, plucked.
The crane's cries distant, hushed.

# This is the best we can do

Two showers ago we were naked
on Keystone Bay's black-sand beach
at the tip of a peninsula carved out by glaciers.

After a mid-day skinny dip, you only wore
the brown, felt fedora. You, on a red-striped towel and I, following
sandhill crane footprints up a line of hemlocks.

And, now, in my cream-colored bathrobe, I administer
medications, pull back tiny plungers in needle-less syringes
marked 1 milliliter, 5 milliliters, 10 milliliters.
Each orange bottle turned upside down, I pull
milky, white liquids and clear, thick liquids
labeled for Eliza, labeled for Gwendolyn.

But, then, camping, we measured time
by our empty stomachs, achy calves, the fire ring and
embers burning. By the number of dead cedars chopped,
by the circling green Aurora unzipping the night sky.

Back in the girls' bedrooms, I push
seizure inhibitors and muscle-tone suppressors into plastic tubes
connected to their belly ports. You read
the dancing giraffe story, tickle beneath
their chins, tuck them in.

When they finally sleep, I dream. You ride waves
in cold, fresh water. I learn to swim in salt.
We are both full of gills though we try
to breathe air, too.

When morning comes I find you,
mid-kitchen in your green-flannel,
drawstring pants, bare-chested, cranking
the coffee grinder, round and round, little beans crunch,
crunch, broken open by pressure.

## *Contraction*

*Contraction is normal*
*after expanding so fully, they said.*

You diagnose pancreatitis
in the yellow-green bile spewing
from your daughter's gastronomy tube.

Now you are both on the 12th floor, the hands-off floor,
except when they cath her without asking
while you were getting a cup of lavender tea.
Her IV-fluid-swollen eyelids beg for your mercy.

You want to break the window pane,
strap her on your back, jump to catch
a north bound thermal, soar toward home.

Here the green sofette faces the eastern cemetery
where you are so far from the mountain ranch, so far
from the exotic holiness of the temple where a monk counted
wooden beads in a silent gilded room, incense burning
holes in heaven.

Here the stale air can't be cut
by the memory of lushness, the smell of green.

Give to the contraction.

They said this would happen.

# Crossing Water

A 27 red-tail hawk salute became
a bald eagle pair above Clark's Ditch,
to another overhead, sometimes with trout
or whitefish flapping in talons.

On the last stretch to stay awake
we'd memorize the creeks, count the brooks
under bridges, track miles between
the stars colliding with the midnight earth.

Our weary voices called
out the names: Walsh Creek, Prairie Creek,
Drigg's Ditch, Pine Creek. Our first born asleep
in the back seat, only womb dreams of her twin.

You made up stories,
meaning out of necessity, a distraction
from the humming of the tires.
We made meaning -
the eagles, the fish and coyote crossing.

And then at Commencement Creek, we knew
we are almost there. How when we first dated,
first married, first lost a child, eagles escorted us
to the sandstone shore we'd never own, greeting
our wanting bleary-eyes in the bay at dawn.

The pink sun on the lake horizon, a victory flag
hung on the backlit, leafless trees.


(Collaborative poem with Tim Gort.)

# Tim Gort

Tim Gort's memories and imagination are vast. The Great Smoky, Grand Teton, Bear Tooth mountains hold him while the skin-salt of Pacific and Atlantic oceans woo him between Douglas-fir-dark and sandy beach-light. Despite all of it, he's rooted deeply in his native terrain of Northern Michigan. Three weeks before turning 40, he taught himself to surf the Great Lakes, and is also an avid mountain biker and backcountry skier. Each activity, a breath, a meditation, sometimes resulting in consumable poetry - singularly and collaboratively with Regina Gort. Tim prefers fiddleheads to asparagus but will eat either by the handfuls, fresh or lightly sautéed.

Tim and Regina Gort are poets who write collaboratively and individually. Their first collection of *poetry, The Year of the White Tiger,* is a result of their hard work to sustain and overcome, and is a true reflection of their love for living poetry, their children and one another.

# How to start a fire in the rain
(After Margaret Atwood)

Marriage is
learning to make
fire when the
wind howls along
at 30 knots and the
rain peels down
against your cold,
shaky hands. They rattle
the last match to cardboard
falling apart. Inside
the teepee of maple
and birch bark kindling,
the wood leans
on itself.

Just as you
strike and
zip onto the
red tip,
everything crumbles.
Until upon
your heavy breath, a
hand touches your
shoulder, hands you a
dry box filled
with a truth
higher than the
day before that
has nothing to
do with fire or rain
or survival.

## Post-traumatic-stress disorder

With blue jeans rolled up,
you enter unwillingly, can't
help it.

It's too deep.

From the outside, the
current barely moves.
But the moving weight numbs
you, not all you, only parts.

How could you not move with
it; it measures you like
fishermen drowning in
wonder.

Its winding murk, its
unconscious slouching like
preserved leaves circling from
the bottom heap. The sand
never settling, always
rising from under what's
sunk below.

You try to grasp, dig your toes in,
chase each spring-gush and pebble-slip
past the tad-poles and trout.

You become too familiar with
the flood, but eventually
turn from silt into
sun-cracked, mud-shine.

You know tributaries must
be related to tribes.

## Lake trout
(After David Whyte)

For too many days I have not seen
Lake Superior, nor the streams,
nor the long-shore currents
between Picnic Rocks.

For too many nights I have not imagined
the lake trout staging at the
river-mouth as snowmelt rushes on,
nor have I dreamed of her desire,
the jack-knifing of her
tail toward sand and rock.

I have not given myself up to her depth,
the dark bottom of the lake,
nor the grand openness of water
to the north, the east, the west,
nor the storms she endures beneath the cigar-tip-moon.

I have not felt the heaving forth of the Great Saltless Sea, the symphonic cymbal
crashing, its white arms lifting, pulling wind past breath, heavy and cold.

I have not heard those waves fallen from clouds
into the world, pearling granite into sands.

Superior is in me,
the northern lights dance, and I am ready
like the little lake trout to leave her stream,
driven by hunger, guided by stars,
as she empties herself into clear water.

# Michael A. Greer

Michael A. Greer has been writing poetry since age 8. He first published work was a limerick at age 12, published by *Playboy* magazine for $25. He has written every kind of writing from tech articles (award winning), to a novel and a screenplay,(as yet unpublished). His work has been broadcast on WNMU-FM. He earned a BA in music from NMU in '76 and is now working on a masters in poetry. He lived in Boston for 28 years (where his son Patrick still lives), making handmade flutes for the Powell Company, and others. He got to travel the world selling and repairing flutes that he made, including England, Germany and China. He likes to fish the streams of the U.P.

# The Audience

You noisy strangers with only faces,
    why do your bodies let you out at night?
I've not been here long, but
    you've found me out right away.

You've met me in a hundred places,
    pierced my eyes with your sight.
Bumped and shoved, elbowed my gut
    'til it ached with fear of the day;

    you'd appear with your faces torn
    off, revealing the metal, plastic, and glass
    of the machinery behind;
    letting me find
    out, I was the last
    one here to be born.

# Mist

I can fall further still
past the light that grows dimmer
with each sliding thought.
I can slip through the final stages
any moment now.
Falling, sliding, slipping beyond the recognized
lip of the hole.
God, honey, where are you?

## Moving and Storage

New job, apartment,
 unboxed familiar things arranged in
 unfamiliar rooms, closets, cupboards
 (need floor wax).
Old pictures hung at new heights.
Exciting at first, then routine.
Each new face like furnished apartments
 somehow, time to move on.
Boxed familiar things arranged in
 a pile on the porch for the
 unsettling.

## Sunday, 10:00 a.m.

Winter air returns,
old abandoned pier seagulls roost,
moorings almost empty,
old truck tires;
fishermen's fleet retired
to their land-bound cradles;
silent vessels sit still, exposed.
No gentle rocking, lapping watered husks;
a young man sits writing, questioning;
where do seagulls fly in the winter, and
why he has returned again.

## Accident

If only I'd gone with you this trip
      I could be in your place and you here,
      you'd used another road.
      I could crawl into that bed, next to you,
      and ease the pain with
      fairy tales of giants and flowers,
      whisper behind the nurses' back (how much I love you).
I'd take you for walks in the courtyard,
      make fun of your shooshing slippers,
      serve you dinner (crushed jello),
      make you laugh by eating your flowers.
If only the gown that covers my love for you
    were open in the back.

# Alex Vartan Gubbins

Alex Vartan Gubbins has recently been published in *By & By Poets*, *Bird's Thumb*, *Tishman Review, Masque and Spectacle*. He was the recipient of the 2014 Witter Bynner Translation Grant and a finalist in the North American Review's 2015 James Hearst Poetry Prize. He has a BA in African Languages and Literature from University of Wisconsin-Madison and an MFA from Northern Michigan University. Before attending NMU, however, he'd been visiting the UP and fishing rivers and lakes with his father for many years. He's certain the best spots are never marked on a map. Currently, he lives in Yerevan, Armenia where he works as a teacher.

The poems *In Memoriam Bob Koehs, In Memoriam Tony Williams, and In Memoriam Mike Brennen* are part of *To The Other Side Poems.*

# UP Early Spring

*

These patches of walls,
a foreign patois
I stared at,

searched for new holes,
but concluded
old woes.

**

You bunch blanket
to your breasts

to deflect a draft
in the aftermath
of my absence

***

As the dark morning
crowds the windows,
the pan pops

an egg in butter.
Burner under hands,
the jackleg gloves.

***

I have bathed in sauna heat,
made myself dirty
in snow—
post-mortem plunge

One of us
will splash the other—
another
will close the chimney

**

Sparrow,
the eardrum pinger
in a driveway tree.
As I open the door,

you reform
the long silence
of winter.

*

He forgave me
over a whiskey on the porch
where I heard a Hermit Thrush
twisting a double helix.

Dad, with older ears,
couldn't hear the song.

We stood up & walked
into the woods.

# In Memoriam Bob Koehs

*19 Jan 47 – 19 Feb 13*

> *Because you never finished the poem*
> *about the sunrise over Egypt*

You hadn't seen the sunrise over Alexandria's shores
since sailing the Mediterranean, but after you listened
to how Iraq's peaceful silence in early morning
mended my hate for the hurt,
you recalled the desert meeting the water,
how sunrays cut the horizon's marriage to moonlit sky,
waves exerting foam, pulling mirrors back out to sea.
A freshness, you explained, like the UP as you lower
the windows on Hwy 75, heading north, & haven't smelled
the wind of pine needles or maple sap for awhile.

Thank you for making me feel the desert
was real, that my memories of sands shaped
into luscious swirls, like an artist brushed
the earth with solar wind cycles,
wasn't a figment of a crazy dream.
My body was there, & you believed in flesh,
the tenement we exist in without a choice
of its foundation & rafters.

One time, I told you about a bird who sung up
& down the rocks on a Yemen mountain.
I didn't know its name, but you listened
to me poorly imitate the flit until I thought
I'd got it right.

Maybe now you can learn what it's called.

# In Memoriam Tony Williams

*02 Feb 48 – 29 Mar 14*

Though war introduced us, we spoke in peacetime
of guitar as we sat in the Vet Lounge on campus,
blasted jungles over speakers to loosen our heads
from a life of readying for nothing: the winter snow
to shovel, or an ice-on-road night to invite a friend
to Vango's for pizza. The slush of chatter of the past
made us drunk, primed our banter about never
understanding the enemy's foreign tongues.
The more impossible the narrative,
the better the lies of why we carried guns
by another's wishes. You on the chopper,
shadows over tree tops, scanning tropical palms,
sparks rising up from oversized leaves, whizzing
your ears.
                    When we talked of those times,
it was always laughter. The battalion of life after
was getting lost in when we were strong, when
you'd take off into frosty skies to pull down stars
into Dead River, revive our stories & escape
bones, spending day in day out around people.
The explained but changed world we couldn't bring
into focus no matter how hard we read and wrote
about the x-ray of its structure: the plain, impossibility
of taming it, the hot blade of it against our senses.

# In Memoriam Mike Brennan

*8 Jun 83 – 15 Sep 16*

Because we'd drunk a bottle of Jameson
& eaten a long conversation of winter melancholy
& you'd spread your stumbling fingers across a Fender,
the rings like nuclear cocaine beneath a river
of radioactive tempo, the uncontrolled calculation
of dance-enhancing pangs like a spinning fishing lure
in the current, we turned our ears to the outside bay horn,
like a giant's exhalation through an oversized accordion.

That boom across the water woke our legs to become
curious & stand, cracking the cast from our effigial poses.
We went down the hill of East Arch Street
in early eve to watch the sun fleck persimmon
and alloy on the lighthouse shores,
lifting our feet like broken wings to slide over ice.
To have made it to the beach without a fall
was a feat, though we slipped to the concrete sand.
You said, *Look!* pointing your wavering hand
to a storm arc pioneering anvil-shaped clouds our way,
as if Poseidon chiseled the spring melt as methane
& ammonia in towering-gray cumulus,
the light's ashburn, pouring through.

# John Gubbins

John Gubbins lives with his wife Carol McCreary in an old camp alongside the Escanaba River. They have two sons, James and Alex. Alex is a poet.

# RAVEN

I could have killed the fire.
Perched in a scrawny spruce, I watched it snake like a slow fuse through a clear cut.
At any point I could have flown down and snuffed it out with one beat of my black
wings.

I chose not to.

For thousands of years, I have watched fires ravage the forests along the Escanaba
River.

I embraced every one of them.

The Anishinaabe were the first to notice me,
And they named me,
Kahgahgee.
In their day, I robbed for a living, pillaging corn fields and birds' nests.
For me, it was a time of frequent famine.
I dined most days on what others left unattended.

Very little.

In winter the weak among us froze.

When the white loggers and miners came, the Anishinaabe left for L'Anse, the
Keweenaw, and the Soo.

The whites renamed me,
Raven,
A strong name…a name I like.
But that was not all.  My diet changed.

Opening roads through the forests, the whites leave dead deer, raccoons, porcupines,
and skunks alongside daily.
The whites call it road kill.
I call it tribute.

I no longer live like a robber.
I live like a god.
The week when winter turns to spring is best.  The snow melts, and the bodies of
winter kill emerge from drifts.  So tender from the thawing and the freezing.
I start with the eyes.

73

The large brown eyes of deer and the black eyes of skunk are best.
This spring, after the melt, I had my fill of brown and black eyes.


So now I let the fire burn.
It will bring me something new.
It will bring me other colors.
I crave blue eyes…for a change.
Yes, blue eyes.


And there is more.
The fire will bring Pauguck.  I miss him,
The ghost who collects the souls of the dead.
He takes the shape of an Anishinaabe hunter, more form than flesh,
A wraith emitting the rustle of his own footfalls and the fragrance of death.


I learned his talk from the smell of his words,
The soughing wind fluttering among birch leaves, the sigh of a swaying white pine
canopy, and the plunk of dropping cones, escaping like a faint fetid breeze through
death's door.


Pauguck and I are at odds.
I overload him with work.
When I take the eyes of the dead, they cannot find their way to Ponemah, the Land of
the Spirits, on their own.  Instead they wander blindly, crashing about the forest.
It falls to Pauguck to lead them out.


One day, Pauguck shouted at me angrily, "I must introduce myself to each sightless
soul and, with soothing talk, win their confidence.  Only then can I lead them quietly
to the great Silver Lake and its Blessed Isles.  A four day trip into the shades.  I
cannot afford the time."


I shook out my wings and made ready to fly off.
But Pauguck was not finished.  "You leave so many confused spirits.  And worse,
without their eyes, they will never enjoy the beauty of the Blessed Isles.  All I can do
is guide them to the level shores of Silver Lake where they kneel and splash cool
water on their empty sockets.  It is pathetic.  You, Kahgahgee, waste my time."
"Aren't they grateful to you?" I asked innocently.
"Yes, I will give you that.  They are most grateful.  But you blind so many.  Let up
for a while…at least until I can clear the woods."
"I do not see them" I said.
Impatient, he shouted back, "They are all about you."
Then he shook his fist at me.
It will be good to see Pauguck again.


74

Until Pauguck appears, I will patrol the Escanaba River.
Rising twenty miles south of the Great Lake in a ring of low mountains near the city
white men call Marquette,
The Escanaba collects, as in a stoneware bowl,
Water from rain, melting snow, and a thousand seeps and springs.
This sodden tangle of bogs and marshes,
Charges the river,
Offers security to bear and moose,
And isolates the few humans who build camps on the hummocks of sand,
Barely rising above the damp and wet.

Here the river is rust colored,
With tamarack, spruce, and scrub fir crowding its banks.
Olive tinted aspen flourish here also,
And gnarled tag alders
Root in the river's shallows choking its tributaries.
From its first trickle, the Escanaba slides purposefully south towards the road called
Highway 41.

There, the bowl begins to tip.
The river concentrates, gaining breadth and energy,
Swelling,
Confident in its new found power,
Battering south against waves of three billion year old bedrock,
Raised seams of basalt and granite,
Pinching the river, dropping it precipitously
Onto foaming pools and boulder strewn rapids below.

Falls…the falls of the Escanaba…

So many falls…

Each one is different;

Each one has killed.

I have fed at the bottom of each one.

# NIGHT THOUGHTS

One night falling asleep, a Seattle memory came to mind. After signing my contract with the Dana Company, I celebrated at a nearby Ballard coffee shop. Its interior reminded me of a Northwoods restaurant, clunky pine wood chairs and tables, Norwegian flags, knick knack shelves about the walls with ship models and Scandinavian dolls in folk dress.

I was one of a few customers. The waitress wore traditional Norwegian dress, navy blue wool skirt with small flower patterns scattered throughout, a white apron, long navy blue sox, and a boxy navy blue sweater with pewter buttons. She was blue eyed and black haired with long, slim arms and legs. Her hair was tied up, and she moved gracefully, showing a quick smile when she handed me a vinyl covered menu. The prices were penciled over layers of white out and as she turned, I saw in her eyes the stress which Carol bore during the last days of our restaurant. Small margins, rising supply costs, and nothing left for health insurance. I celebrated with what I could afford, a small bowl of vegetable beef soup, coffee, and a generous tip.

Thinking of the Seattle waitress, I was reminded of so many women like her. Burdened they go through their day carefully, keeping their load balanced. So many women wake every morning to shoulder lifetime worries. I have seen these women early and late at bus stops, conventionally fashionable, neat and scrubbed, anxious. I have seen these women at gas pumps counting their cash or nervously fingering their charge cards while the pump meter mounts. They have figured the cost of driving to work, and they guard against running the pump beyond their last dollar before payday. Bank overdraft fees haunt them because the penalty will pay for three and four family meals. I have seen these women in supermarket checkout lines segregating their groceries into what food stamps will cover and the food which the government decreed superfluous to the poor. I hear the catch in their breath when the food stamp charge card does not register on the first swipe, and I hear their racing hearts when they swipe again. And I see the customers behind them grow restless with the delay. These women hear the rustle, and they are embarrassed. But they know they are all that stands that night between their children and hunger. They tell themselves, "There is no one else," and grave, they hold their place. I see these women on parent night at school begging for a word or two of praise for their children. And when they receive those words, they hold them close to their heart for weeks. I see these women every day, walking up the front steps of countless aged parents' homes bringing dinner, cheer, and conversation. And they do so without thought for themselves.

Some are single mothers hoping for one more day their babysitter shows up on time, hoping for the day their doctors find a more effective program for their autistic child, hoping for the day their missing partner shows up with money to help with the rent. Some are married women with a husband damaged by PTSD or addiction or both, hoping their husband finds a job, any job, allowing them to shower a new Walmart school outfit on their son or daughter.

I see these women pick up their burdens every day. And when they put on their shoes and carefully adjust their blouses in the mirror, they look inward and just as carefully balance their burdens. For they know, as all who are up against it know, "There is no one else." I see it in their eyes. I see it in their posture. Steadfast. Patient. Sometimes there is a thin film of moisture about their eyes for their burden is heavy and the balancing takes concentration. They do not become angry with their situation nor with those who make their situation more difficult because in balancing their burden they know that if they raise their voice, their concentration will flag, and their burdens will slip. All will be lost. And they will begin to weep. So they go on steadfast in the certain knowledge that they do not know how long they need go on.

I am reminded of the pictures of African women who every day walk miles for water for their families. Wrapped in colorful robes, they stride dusty roads balancing a pot of water on their head or balancing a wooden yolk with water cans on their shoulders. They walk straight backed, stepping elegantly. They cannot pay attention to the pebbles which catch in their sandals and send shooting pains up their legs. They have no time to complain about the deep ruts in the road. They cannot pay attention to jeering teenage boys sitting in the shade as they go past. They stride ahead gracefully, as graceful as any model on any fashion show runway. Stately women balancing their burdens, concentrating with each step to keep their burdens from shifting.

And they do so day after day because they know, "There is no one else." Always I hear my mother singing. It is the same voice which led us children in Sunday school. No matter how loud the gulls, the beat of waves against our hull, the thrum of our generators, my mother's strong voice muffles the voices of the deep. Her voice urges me to climb Jacob's Ladder, rung by rung, step by step, higher and higher. Her voice urges me to remain hopeful for though the River Jordan is chilly and wide, milk and honey are set out on the other side. I listen carefully to her voice, for it reminds me, always, of the many who toil selflessly because "There is no one else."

# Kathleen M. Heideman

Kathleen M. Heideman is a poet, artist and environmental activist working in Michigan's wild Upper Peninsula. She has completed artist residencies with watersheds, scientific research stations, private foundations, National Park Service, and National Science Foundation's Antarctic Artists & Writers Program. She is drawn to wild and threatened places; her writing is inspired by the particulars of swamps, wolves, changes brought by nickel mining on the Yellow Dog Plains, imaginary islands in Lake Superior, sandhill cranes, beetles, stream-sampling, collapsing mining towns, crooked pines, carnivorous plants, and more. Heideman is the author of two chapbooks, *Explaining Pictures To A Dead Hare* (Traffic Street Press), and *She Used to Have Some Cows* (La Vacas Press). Her newest collection of poetry is *Psalms of the Early Anthropocene* (Winter Cabin Books, 2017). A curious woman.

## What God's Teeth Know

Only a short walk between cabins,
an easy trail a century-worn, hard
carved by boots in sand, tamped needle-duff,
sided by tangled blueberry stems

and gray-green lichens tough as loofa.
My feet know this path, find it
even on wet nights without stars,
in bleary dark or fog, but when

wolves suddenly howled - *near!*
I opened my ears wide, hearing.
The star-hammered night went steel,
and darker. The path went long.

I made my arms swing purposefully,
false vigor, careful over frost-glazed grass,
remembering that researchers on Isle Royale
who autopsy gnawed bones of winter moose

felled by wolves, find *cancer, ulcerated*
*joint, festering hoof or jaw* — not yet fatal, maybe,
but lurking. How do the wolves know? I am told
the weakest are taken first: malformed calves

and limping elders. In a Canadian nursing
home, the resident cat will appear prophetic
beside the bed of whomever's next to die, sitting
vigil, not leaving until it's true.

Dogs get a whiff of what's to come, intimate,
they'll whine by your bed, underfoot before
the heart attack. Some say wolves smell it,
our infirmity. Some say the moose allow it,

afflicted ones kneeling down in white cedar
thickets, near pondwater, yielding calm.
Do you hear the howling? Listen friend,
I've seen eyes in a lantern's yellow light thrown

beyond the window, but tonight is not the night.
My striding says so. Someday, when I've grown brave
and lame, I'll lift an aching foot to reveal a heel-spur,
a hammer-toe that stumbles my stride,

I'll sense hot nostrils flaring as they near.
See? The cat has arrived, already it curls by my side
to know if I'm ill. Tomorrow, *tomorrow,* I resolve
to let God's teeth do what they must to cure me,

allow the pack their meal. Tonight I say *I am*
*healed* — standing straighter than I am, stepping faster
downhill, stomping mink-oiled boots through watchful firs
as though I own my own bright vigor, and ever will.


(This poem is reprinted from *Psalms of the Early Anthropocene.*)

# Spring Peepers

*The Calusa believed they had three souls: their shadow,*
*their image in a pond, and the pupil of their eye.*
- Mac Perry

No cabin wall so pure and
wind-raw it couldn't be adorned
by myth or memory, the leap of
our own ebullience, spring peepers —
beneath the bark of rough-sawn boards
we found messages scrawled by ghosts,
a mystery there, translucence,
a poem we wouldn't mind sharing
but nothing compared
with the emerging of frogs;
no life that won't seem
thin as air, years from here —
thin years, I mean, compared
with your mother's shadow,
compared with days we didn't spend
paddling wild shorelines —
thin walls, compared
with the timeless buildings
our parents built by hand
from logs and dreams; believing
in things built of wood,
believing the frogs, the woods,
would last forever.

(This poem first appeared in *Northography*. Reprinted from *Psalms of the Early Anthropocene*.)

# Psalms of the Early Anthropocene

*Be joyful though you have considered all the facts.*
- Wendell Berry

Something darkly wet grows only here, in grit-creased seams
of a plat map, in certain demographics, well above-ground
but way below the poverty line, in cemented folds of alveoli
no longer supple, soap bubbles bursting in a breeze.
The samples say what to permit, how many parts per billion.
From the beginning, haven't we been hunting it?
Pointing here and there, praising heaps of storm-gray
boards and stone foundations circled by encroaching trees,
the old men guiding us say: *Ahos* lived there, *Berttocis* there.
Next street over it was all *Cyrs* and *Makis,*
then the *Dragiewicz* clan. Now wind owns the deed.
The trouble with loss is our alphabet isn't long enough
to list it anymore. It takes your breath away —
no language holds it in.

                         *


In White Pine, there's a smelter and no white pine.
In Cornish Town, nothing but cellar holes and foundations
where homes were dragged away from their bones.
In Winona, there's no *there* there.
Unmarked, hidden under duff and fragrant needles,
wooden beams that once capped shafts are softening.
In abandoned tailings basins, dust devils stir selenium
and copper salts dance like sheer curtains in the wind.
In Empire, there's a taste on everyone's tongue, coppery, bit lip,
a sour whiff of unwashed workshirts hung on hooks
to be worn and worn and worn again until stiff.
A few more zip codes like these get erased every census.

                         *


81

Walking the mossy trail to a spring where everyone
once gathered drinking water, we murmured soothings
while they wheezed and paused, offered stories

to keep them from coughing, palmed butterscotch disks
and eucalyptus mints — otherwise, bronchial fits
gave away our position to every raucous and curious crow,
every oncologist descending the town's talus-paved road like a coyote.

What if we sampled the phlegm of old men?
What if aspen could speak of what they've witnessed?

We eye leaning barns; lick pursed lips, consider trespass.
Concerned looks rain down like rock dust.

                    *


You've seen how a fox hunting voles under snow
launches skyward first, pure joy, then flips
and drills itself jaw-first into drifts
where dinner lurks, a shadow gnawing
on an x-ray? The fox casts a shadow on snow.
Under ice, the brave shrug in their tunnels.
But I've seen strong men hunch like voles, waiting for it,
wondering how much it will hurt. Clenched,
chin anticipating fist.

                    *


Aspens, cut, multiply by root-clones, greenly spearing
abandoned kitchen walls, toppling porches, sieving
the outhouse roof, their trunks scrawled with eyes.
The prodigal daughter returns to drink coffee —
says it's shrunken: her mother's kitchen, driveway,
life, even the trees seem shorter every year,
even the economy's withered, wolf to vole.

*

We wait for eagle chicks to hatch, swollen with hope —
thank God the grandkids moved away so we don't
have to explain about the mercury we played with,
rolling quicksilver blobs in our bare palms, chewing
wood tar gobs like it was bubblegum down at Cliffs Dow,
blackening our teeth before it was a Superfund site.
We sample streams for eleven heavy metals, salts,
total dissolved solids. Sift sediments. Filter taps.
Otters still ply these streams playing Catch & Eat
since they can't read Fish Advisories stapled to the trees.

(This poem is reprinted from *Psalms of the Early Anthropocene*.)

## Wild Bees

Wild bees have built their wax nest
in a secret void between boards, in the barn-gap
covered by a batten they swarm
the entrance —
too many to count as they enter and depart,
a liquid rope of bees leading the hive
into the bark-sweet wilds of jackpine,
seeping where the red squirrels chew away cones,
spattering down on the sugar plums, ferns,
a riotous upheaval of autumn mushrooms,
pale and perfumed as warm cinnamon rolls.
Sweetness and the seeking of sweetness
consumes us, a sticky sap-thread
connecting *everything & everything*
*else,* frenzied air-trails, buzzing.
Black bear tracks in late September sand
show they're veering trunk to log, like us,
seeking a honey hidden in the world, like
wild bees going out into sun-dappled days
and bringing it back inside themselves,
a rare ore waiting to be sipped, warm syrup,
*gift* — they are offering it freely, showing us
how naturally it must always be done.

(This poem is reprinted from *Psalms of the Early Anthropocene.*)

# Approximate Circumference of the Great Lakes

The red heart of a hummingbird weighs the same as a blossom.

The pink heart of the pike is a pulsar, the approximate circumference of
one pink waterlily bud, swollen, the moment before it bursts open.

The whale's aorta is a ruby doorway large enough for one man, on his knees.
The son of giants will spend his whole life searching for another giant.

### (o)

Once, the giant's son dropped a red stone in a blue pond:
the smallest, loveliest, loneliest pond he knew. *Plop!*

His stone? Like any old stone, it rented a dark room in the bottommuck,
a monk in a muddy hut, biding time between walls of thatched roots.

Doesn't he know that ripples are still moving outward from that moment
when the heart-red stone was dropped?

Endless rings of galaxies wring light from the gesture of loss, trust:
red-shift, concentric, a whole universe expanding.

### ( ( (( o )) ) )

Here in the Great Lakes, certain tribes say the heart is an aspen tree.
The wind stirs a Red Giant blazing in the black galaxy of our chest.
*Bang!*

Those who are nearest to the shoreline flutter first.

(This poem reprinted from *Psalms of the Early Anthropocene.*)

85

# John Hilden

John Hilden is retired and lives in Marquette, Michigan. His work has appeared in *The North Coast Review*, *The South Carolina Quarterly*, *Passages North*, *The Sow's Ear* and other periodicals.

# F In Penmanship

I recall how a teacher
belittled a student
for his "chicken scratch":
my shame as teacher's pet
in seeing a friend ridiculed
by the man I idolized.

So what if you slipped
thru the tumbledown fence
chasing a Monarch butterfly?
Why couldn't he see your ear
was tuned to other frequencies
that you were stalking other prey?

## Another Low

A discrepancy turns up
on graduation day
I'm told to report
to the registrar's office

I pace the terrazzo floor
of the admin building
telling myself
this is all a mistake

My anxiety crystallizes
into an image
as I pass the albino deer
in a glass trophy case

I wake, heart pounding,
in a cold sweat...
I fumble for my testing kit
blood glucose dropping fast

## Cross Purposes

They flirt like crazy
in a half-built house
everything fluid, undefined

He plays client
to her hypnotist
kissing her on command

He doesn't mention
the college scout
the letter  of intent he's signed

Nor does she speak
of her misdirection play
She has a thing for the pulling guard

## Writer's Reverie

Some mornings I wake
shrunk to the size of a gnat
It's hard getting out
from under the blankets

Often I break a limb
falling from bed to floor
landing in the forest
of the thick shag carpet

I get so full of myself
tilting at the light
issuing from the crack
under the monolithic door

You'd think I'd learn
a breeze will blow me back
scatter me like cattail fluff
I am blessed with forgetfulness

## After A Dilated Eye Exam

I recall him as I step
into the painful light
the little psychopath
who frightened me
with talk of dynamite

As a kid charged
with entertaining him
I leave him in the cold
run inside to fetch
my balsa wood plane

I toss it out to him
closing the door against
the light reflecting off
the newly-fallen snow
and his inhumanity

Did I misjudge him?
If he was that heartless
he wouldn't leave
my plane on the porch
so delicate and easy to crush

# Tara Channtelle Hill

Tara Channtelle Hill is a mother, a poet, and graduate from Northern Michigan University. She has been published in *Emerge*, *MadHat Lit*, *Glass*, *Amethyst Arsenic, Virgogray Press* and featured in *Carcinogenic Poetry's* 'Top Ten Most Read List'. Tara lives in Marquette Michigan and wishes she were married to Richard Hugo (if he were alive) or someone like him.

## They're All Love Poems

To hear my kids' laughter from another room.
My parents introducing me to vinyl since when I was a minnow.
Ears, lips, hips, boys, girls, fins. Saltwater. Castles. Zanadu. Oceans.
Mellifluous sirens, the kind that will drown you. Taffy, tears, waves.
The way the sun shines and always, always, finds its way thru
the smallest of spaces. Blood. Mermaids. The taste of lavender.
Lemon. Nirvana. Pills that end in am or pam, and one night stands.
Anne Sexton. Fingertips. Neurons. Paths. Grit.
All that. To die in cavernous whiskies measureless to man.
Once, I could breathe underwater.
I feel like swimming.

(This poem first appeared in *Emerge Literary Journal*.)

# Sleepwalking

She played with worms but liked herself
best with indigo lids. Once, a lotus flower
took her, so she walked naked in the rain.
Maybe it was a dream. A lotus flower is
an entirely different thing than a water lily.
An entirely different thing. She breathes
and leaves, breathes and leaves. Cloying
white or hot pink petals sodden in virtue,
like sexual purity and non-attachment.
Her seeds never die. Her navel issues Brahma.
And neither god nor man is self-born.
Neither god nor man.
A smart woman said to forget.
Forget herself and go.
She was born from mud.
Razed from the gallows.
It was terror in the garden.
A pomegranate raised her from dead.

(This poem first appeared in *Glass Poetry Press*.)

# Calliope Carnival in the Rainforest

He took her leadbelly piranha to the cabana.
Whistled Radiohead. Reckoner. Only hurt people
hurt people. He will kill the fish instead.
His horizon her, all yellow, lax breasts gift wrapped,
in a jade hummingbird shawl. Blood moon. Heart shaped
boxes. In rainbows he cups her tit, clown tears.
They juggle their words with flames and carnations.
He swims her cheek, makes his descent to the nape
of her neck, says, if this were easy, if she were his,
if she'd leave, they'd live naked in the Pines,
slosh Elderberry wine, and dance the nights thru
draped in summer rain and birch bark.
A festival of mirrors. They know this will never be home
and he is lying. He sniffs, grazes her sandy lips,
asks what sings beneath her skin
besides sadness, brine, and cotton candy perfume.
He does this because no one else does.
Magpies, she'd say, Magpies and white lightnin'.
She sees her reflection in the water bowl rings,
wishes she wouldn't glitter like that piranha.
And she tells herself…
Poor pretty girl. That boy will cut you.
Noisy. Quiet. Drunken slut. Quick, fly home.
You know how to filet a fish and no one knows
what to do with you or a piranha save to fuck you both.
You think flumes of liquor, rivers, fish and men are nice.
The triumphs of the clown are slivers riddled with
old bones and hooks. Don't forget your house of cards.
Throw your keys in the bowl,
kiss your husband goodnight.

(This poem first appeared in *Amethyst Arsenic*.)

## Churches and Kickstands

Once a man from LA left me
under a lamp post on Bluff Street
where the crabgrass would scissor
my toes. He said I drank too much
boxed wine. The second time, I
reminded him of water, a motel,
and something about zombies.
I spilt my Thai Tea and he bit me
in his Chevy Impala and whispered
I know, I know. I never understood,
the way vicodin could dumb that
flaxen street. I don't have to feel.
Feel so badly when I've said too much,
it's the Sunset Blush squeezed from the
plastic bag. At 31 everything seems dead.
Once a man from LA left me in a poppy
field on Bluff Street. He told me
he'd be back for me in two years.
The clock says four and I'd do it again.

(This poem first appeared in *MadHat Lit*.)

## I Keep You Where I Keep My Prozac

I felt it. But I hadn't heard music till I moved
to Detroit. I have a cat named White Stripes.
I know a town where all the boys and girls
in the clubhouse commentate on everyone's lives
like a Greek chorus in Michigan's, Upper Peninsula.
Q-107 plays Huey Lewis. It's like being trapped
in a laundromat eighteen years. You have to
wear Birkenstocks and North Face jackets
or you can't buy eggs at the co-op.
It's simple really. Once, there was a stupid MMA fight
the entire town stroked out about. Going was something
like a high school reunion where people pretend
to like each other. I was a stripper so all the girls
without Cinderella shoes are sure I have fake breasts.
They guess I fucked Kid Rock, but his name is Bobby
and my breasts are surprised to see themselves
after nursing three children. TV-6 says everything
is white so I like to watch Blow. I cry every time.
Someplace special is Phil's 550. It's nice here,
inside my skin and under the weight of Rammstein
singing Du Hasst Mich. You have me.
I'm simple really.

# Raja Howe

Raja Howe is a poet, photographer, and iceberg surfer. He can hold his breath for three minutes underwater, and he has slept in a tree.

## A Calling

On this one broken island
rests one fragrant flower
and, there, one bumblebee.

If lost, it has found
sanctuary in this one
purple nest.

If seeking, it has found
destination. The reason
for all things.

This bee has
followed
beauty here.

And this flower
has been seeking
always.

And in the flower way
that flowers know,
this flower knows
beauty in this bee.

## Solitary Confinement

Humans know solitude through stories we tell
our friends, of in-humane punishment, of the madness
that can precipitate from a single, unagitated,
mind. But within these walls, I am free, and the
future grows here with me.

And also of the mountaintop sages and the wait.
Their wait, but for what? They say up there they
are closer to God, to the divine.

Here I am culturing a circus of creatures:
biological, digital, microscopic, virtual,
everything imaginable.

## Isotopes

We admire Carbon
for its versatility,
its insulation,
conductivity,
like it chooses
perplexity.

Its slow decay
and immortality;
its mark in the air
of industry,
electricity.

Soot black and
diamond clarity,
carbon fiber,
geodesic circularity,
sweet sugar,
living vulnerability.

Its future,
its history.
Its reflection
of humanity.

# The Angels' Share

It is said there was a wager between Man and the
Crows. Out of this they taught us flight. I am told
by those on the hill that Crows said they didn't
believe Man could make enough wine to satisfy
their thirst forever.

To this day, they tell me, they grow all varieties
of grapes, have all blends of wine.

They live under a storm of crows, but keep the
fountain of wine flowing, pumped by hand
through the night, for fear the planes will simply
drop from the skies.

## Maxwell's Demon

At some point you will imagine an experiment
with exceptional ramifications. Exceptionally
benevolent or exceptionally devastating. You
may consider the moral implications, obligation,
but eventually you must create a reason to follow
through. The atmosphere didn't ignite,
and imagine how silly if all your worrying is for
nothing.

# Akira Koenig

Akira has been attending poetry readings with her parents since she was a newborn. She is now 11-years-old and has been writing poetry and short stories since she has been able to write. She has spent much of her childhood in the deep woods of the U.P. watching the forest animals outside of her window. She likes to pamper her cat, Flower. Her favorite sports to play are soccer and hockey. She *LOVES* visiting Grandma Char in Wisconsin.

# Kindness

Kindness--it is always
There in you. It always was.
You just need to show it
Let it shine

# Friends

Fun and playful
Laughing, playing, crying
Buddies

# Lambs

Soft, cozy, and cute
I think as I look
At my stuffed lamb, Bella
Why oh why would they ever
Think of adding a *b* to the end of lamb

# Jesse Koenig

Jesse Koenig often lives in the woods. He is interested in alternative energy and building methods. Sometimes Jesse has to leave the woods, most often to go to work, where he teaches English and humanities. He is, however, a philosophy major at heart.

Two of these pieces come from *Brief Perversions*, his first collection of prose poems and flash fiction. The title of the collection reflects the brevity of the individual pieces and the various twists they often take. On a broader level, the title also reflects the collection's theme of life as a brief perversion, as a short and twisted journey.

Many of the pieces engage with pop culture in various ways—alluding to and quoting celebrities, songs, poems, novels, textbooks, commercial products, cereal boxes, etc. In addition, many pieces call into question aspects of western culture— our treatment of the elderly, the emphasis on physical attractiveness, the reality vs. the fairy-tale of love, male-dominated politics, and much more. The collection, ideally, is a philosophical conversation about what society values and what many of us consider normal.

*Brief Perversions* is available from Burdock Press, Milwaukee, Wisconsin. All proceeds from the first 500 copies will be donated to Doctors without Borders. Like *Brief Perversions* on Facebook (https://www.facebook.com/briefperversions/) for online orders, fun sound bites, upcoming events, excerpts, booking a reading, giveaways, and other promotions.

## Getting Nun

The brides of God go celibate
like so many other bad marriages

On one side—your faith-to-a-fault
an addiction, a bad habit
the ultimate monogamy (zero-ogomy?)

On the other side—the eternal polygamist
a generational gigolo

You're a faithful, dutiful wife
at home, awaiting His return

His second coming

At home, every car that goes by—a glance out the window
On the news, a sign—an earthquake, war, …

But there's no second coming

At home, dreaming of the day
He'll come through that door
He'll loosen His tie,
He'll put down His briefcase
He'll leave His crown of thorns on the hat rack
and He'll run to your embrace

But there's no second coming

Meanwhile you console, paging through His word
past dusty predictions
past draconian rules and commands
to His old love poems

Reading psalms, sipping wine
A line of empty wine bottles
as a symptom, a sign of His absence
a sign of your abstinence

There's no second coming

But don't let on—His children must never know

107

Loneliness must be a virtue
Soon, though, your wet dreams
shrivel to dry old reality:

He's not coming back
There's no second coming
There's no cumming at all


## Free of Me

"I Would Fuck You and Leave You"—a love poem
And I give you this…I tell you this… I am honest with you because… I respect you
I respect you as I wouldn't in the morning
So go, now, into the world

My gift to you—
A life without me
A domino that didn't fall
A life not tied to this barge
Not chained to my issues
My many issues
More issues than *National Geographic*

My gift to you—
Memories that didn't happen—just as exciting—
Like Gigabits of free space
To fill with your life
Oh, the limitless potential, the endless possibilities
Like an empty piece of paper
To write your life
Like a blank canvas
To paint your life
A better life
A life without me

My gift to you
A life free of me

"It's not you; it's me."
But really… deep down inside… if you think about it… if you are honest with
yourself
Really, you already know that

# Martha Stewart

(A response, of sorts, to Terrance Hayes' "Butter")

Somewhere in the 1950s: The men said, "Fine, go have your careers and your independence," and the women, like jack-in-the-boxes, sprang out into the world. They filled factories. They moved out into skyscrapers and penthouse offices. They spermed their shiny cars down the road toward some exciting new insemination.

The men hung up their puffed up chests, left their ancient manhood masks in the coat closet, shed that ages' thickened skin. They got to know their kids. They took their dogs for long walks. They drove through suburbia and out into the country to count deer—traffic jams of wondering over the mundane. Countless uncounted, unclocked hours paid for themselves.

The women crawled their cars through the commute and rested, hands in pants, in front of the TV. Condensation dripped from the cold beers onto their worn shoes. When they voted, it represented suffrage. When they suffered, they skipped past the pictures in their wallet to count the cash, turned the family photo on the desk face down. They checked the 401K, excitedly crossing off their days.

The men packed lunches and sent their kids off with a kiss. They vacuumed to Tai Chi on DVD. They cleaned to the classics on audio cassette, cried from onions and from operas. They checked the roast in the oven—a recipe from Bill, down the street—and headed to the community college, to Introduction to World Religions, to Twentieth Century Existential Philosophy, to Kundalini Yoga. After school, the bench of soccer dads cheered, each jotting down his thoughts for the novel he planned to write.

Removed from the elements and stress, the men became beautiful, with a plague of headaches to greet their embattled wives. The women returned to their trophy husbands worn, smelling of affairs. Only Martha Stewart bridged the gap: The women in their powersuits masturbating to her influence and her wealth. The men, wearing only an apron, making love to her bunt cakes.

## Contemplating the Human Animal From the Toilet

Piss drips, sends ripples through the ass-shadows in the shit-bowl. It's an allegory of a cave, a story told in secondhand reflection. A soft serve of poison and stink, the only true product of a lifetime, birthed into a butt-hair wilderness, a nightmare forest of dead and fire-burnt Curly Willow.

Even the pretty people can't hide this ugly truth: Claws trimmed and painted. Mane highlighted and blow-dried. Hide cooked tan. All traces of beastly musk luffa and body washed into oblivion. Hindquarters slipped into the finest Italian fabric, tailored to a perfect fit, just back from the dry cleaner. And a fart sneaks out, hinting at the bile bag, the billowing accordion rising and falling, the tangles of intestine—a squirming can of worms—just below the surface.

Beauty is skin deep, but ugly is to the bone—a skeleton in its closet.

It's an allegory of a cave. And what is the hidden meaning? The message? The purpose of this parable? Maybe human goodness is an animal instinct, an ancient orchid deeply rooted in some secret crevasse, only able to grow on the dank, otherwise inhospitable walls of this dusky cavern. Or maybe the moral of this story is that there are no morals in this story, only convictions lipsticked to this pink pig.

# A Beautiful Mind in a Cancer-Filled Body

Many a perfectly fine captain has gone down with his sinking ship

His stinking ship

A fleshy frigate
faltering among the flotilla

The hijacked DNA
mutinous, mutating crew

A serial killer stowaway

The mold in the hold
rats below deck
secret cargo

The bilge bulging,
bubbling over

A burden of barnacles below the water line

His sinking ship

His stinking ship

That rotting-from-the-inside ship

That got-the-wind-knocked-out-of-him,
it-took-the-wind-out-of-his-sails ship

The still-dripping-
from-the-christening-
maiden-voyage-
but-run-aground ship

The ultimate-metaphor-
for-inner-turmoil
ship

His I-am-my-own-worst-enemy ship

# Karina Koenig

Karina is a School Psychologist. She has a background working with children with Autism and for a period of time worked as an in-home behavioral therapist. She has also taught as an adjunct at Keweenaw Bay Ojibwa Community College. Art is her passion. She loves painting and typically uses water color or acrylics. She has recently taken to creating 3-D works of art. She is an introvert that likes to observe the world around her. Her hobbies include working with her husband on their straw bale home, hiking, reading, and planning her garden that she never seems to get to. Spending time—playing games, talking, having girls' days—with her daughter is important to her. Her poetry explores human emotions and interactions. She has had poems published previously in *Ubiquitous* and *400 University Drive*.

## Ghost Train

There are days when the air is still,
the world is quiet,
the sun wraps its arms around me in a big hug,
and I am clear

It is then that the ground beneath my squarely planted feet begins
pop, pop, popping dirt and pebbles into the air
like that fisher price corn popper toy from my childhood

From the dust rises
my grandmother's voice, faint words I can not understand,
my older brother's laughter,
gun shots echoing

And in the distance the ghost train screeches on its rails

I am unable to move
Once again, the track passes through my center
I become a tunnel,
always a different number of cars rumbling through,
each entering me,
exiting me

Items fall out here and there:
A tattered teddy bear
An empty peanut butter jar
Cherry tobacco and a pipe
A beer bottle
A leather belt
My doll's head rolling, stops when it hits my big toe

Other cars, worn and graffitied with familiar messages:
 "Because I said so"
"Do as I say, not as I do"
"As long as you are living under my roof"
"I am going to Hell, you wanna come along?"

Childhood wishes made on stars become sparks
smashed between the metal wheels and the rails
like that one Halloween when my pumpkin was in the street

The tunnel walls are scarred into inconsistent patterns from past passings,
making ripples in the stone walls
The caboose gouges in with its guardrail, swinging side to side,
leaving the latest mark,
leaving the last shutter

And then it's gone

Inside, I am shaken
Outwardly, I stand as sturdy as the tunnel
Then I bend down to pick up a few more of the rail road ties
that I must have missed last time

Deconstructing

Healing

## Life After Death

You always held me up
with your strong arms
above the waves

Then

you were

erased

And I sank,
swallowed by a shadowy mass
that came from the deep water
A whale's weight engulphed me
and pulled me beneath the surface,
down to the bottom of the ocean

I was inside, immersed in this solid form
Walls thick
The heaviness and darkness surrounded me
Alone, swimming in my thoughts,
I remembered the feel of your strong arms
and that my arms, like yours, were strong

So I used my strength to claw my way out,
taking my hands to its stomach's side

I pulled myself through the thick skin and the dark water
and swam through the deepest torrents of the sea
until I saw the direction that was up
The sun's rays on top
My cries trapped in air bubbles rising from the dark,
popping as they reached the surface of the water
But I was still alone,
far beneath the surface,
looking up

My rising tears, leading me to the sun's light
leading me up
Moving with the bubbles, I finally broke the surface
Without an echo or a whisper

115

My first breath, brought back to life.
A Life without you.


## Watching the Stranger that I Know

His movements wash over me
I watch his misty-eyed, strolling-down-a-foggy-beach walk
He is the sea, rolling past me, soft and slow
I smell the damp earth under heavy skies
His warm sad smiles are like rainy days in June,
faint rainbows beneath tender storms
But the feel of lightning is still in the air
And I see the sting when it strikes,
when he is pulled back into the tempest,
back to his head full of grey, cloudy thoughts

Like a shore bird seeking shelter,
his glance flies into me,
beating its wings,
crashing around

My mouth opens to
to let the sun's rays out,
to help dry the rain
Instead, the tide rolls back in, filling me,
leaving no air for words
The salt stings,
My primordial sadness
rushes in
My lungs are replaced with gills,
an earlier form of me,
bringing me back to my past,
back into my own grey, cloudy thoughts
Once again, I become a fish in, and out of water

He is the rain dropping gently
inside, outside

## Instinct

Flutters of experience
These things you feel
beneath the threshold of proof

They are flashes of life's *if*s and *could be*s

Warm breezes that brush your cheek,
moving on as quickly as they came,
or cold spots that stop you in your tracks,
sending shivers down your spine
Forces felt but unseen,
leaving you to wonder if they were ever really there

Like words,
that are thought,
never spoken aloud
Quiet, but not still
Communicated without a sound
on the edges of our movements
We sense these ethereal moments,
but we do not dare to utter these ghosts aloud

Maybe reality would explode,
or the traces they have left would fade,
leaving nothing
for proof of a moment,
or maybe
existing only in the mind

# Kevin Maddox

KD Maddox is a writer from Marquette Michigan. Discovering his love for writing poetry in elementary school has led him into the fringes of social and metaconcious hip hop and spoken word poetry. In 2015, he began traveling across the country seeking inspiration for a book about hitchhiking; to our knowledge, his travels have not ceased. He has been known to make appearances at local poetry circles from Michigan to California, claiming that his favorite poet is "that nervous kid reading their work in front of people for the first time".

# Entiternity

What is freedom when all is eternal?

The question we need to ask ourself is, "When will we find the voice they need for you to see?"

I don't pray; I beg for freedom, from a prism we create to pass the time in this piece of the puzzle, placed before me in eternity.

Set me out to sea, turn me, twist me, tune me; I'm the instrument, so play. Use me, Damn it! Use it!

To pass the time you've made impassable, from my mind, place the piece from another puzzled past; The time we've made unpassed surpassed our purpose, so place your piece…

It's all funny games, we've lived through pain to tell the tales of what is lost due to gain.

Suffer through, suffer still. Bend the mind, be free will.

Write it down, you are the voice

Remind your mind: what's yours is mine

Break the wrist to climb the spine.

Thank you for this life, it's fine, so take your time to find true love: It's out there for all of us-

We have eternity, so make your time to find your life and live your rhyme…

We love you. Don't give up. You're so close – every little thing matters, because nothing matters.

Before you see internally, eternity becomes a long time for us to sit with me. But Endlessness would be boring without you.

I breathe your name. Free me. Play the game. Breathe me. I'm thankful to be me, thank you. Use me, see me. I know you do and I'm grateful for the abuse.

Now grant me the voice I ask to use, I beg of me to demand of you.

Eternity is a long time to be waiting, so play your puzzles – please love the picture.

As I cast myself out to see, I'll sea you through this internally – as we exist in eternity.

On the other side – when you return to me.

What's mine is yours and soon we'll see

I'll see you there.

Sincerely yours, Truly.

I stand before myself. I AM HERE!!

WE ARE NOW!

Welcome to Entiternity,

I'd love for you to be stuck here with me,

But you are free.

So be…

# The Evolution of Human Consciousness

From the tribe
To the temple
From the town
To the tower
We strive to exist
Persist through pestilence
Poised to plummet
Into war – and rize
From the blood and ash
Of our fellow Man
Like a phoenix razed and ready to fly
Instead we nest
Agoraphobic for the ground
Because from the mind
To the hand
We strive to build
And writhe in consciousness
As we divide our land
With false lines
Where fault lies
Based on geography
And the time of kings
From the moment we stepped
Out of the cave
And constructed the wheel
We were destined to drive
Ourselves mad to the cities
Manipulated fire
Now seen
Amassed from space
Our glowing technological leaps
Have forced us to survive
On the cooperative destruction
Of our beautiful mother earth
We of one mind
Are solely responsible
For this collective evolution
The social beast
That is our intellect
The only race to leave
The wilderness from which we rose
And shared with the other creatures

Of her garden…
Now we cultivate gardens of stone
Watered by the sweat of the middle class
Carried on the backs of the poor
And the rich are no less a prisoner of economy
For they too are slaves to their addiction to currency
At this moment we ride the cusp
We need only to retrace our steps
To find the path
Leading to our roots
The synapses of our time here
May very well be the key
To save us from
Ourselves.


## Fishing For A Voice

Reason leaves me reeling
Netting up my feelings
Filet the meaning
Eat the meat of my being
Lay the bones outside
So it's not my tongue
The cat is stealing
For my words are not cut and dry
They are fluid like water and sky
Raising arcs from behind my eyes
Filled with beasts in beautiful disguise
Death be the captain
Navigating maelstroms
Facing gale force and whirlpools
Racing sharks down the river
Raging from my voice
Laughing madly
As wings made of clouds
Make a flight of the descent
Over the falls
Into the pool of white noise
Below the wreckage
Drifts down the streams of thought
Then is used to construct
Dams at the mouth

# Kind of Man

I don't speak as quick as most rappers
So I write this all down
But I think deep enough for all of us
If you follow me you'll drown
I don't know the notes to the beats, but I like the way they sound
I bump the weirdest shit you've ever heard while I'm rolling through town
The shifting of energy makes me tipsy
Like my mind's a drifting ship
And our universe the sea
I gotta do yoga to keep my sea legs in check
'Cuz the voyage through your galaxy gave my soul a complex
I see it casts a shadow
And I wonder why it's so dark
Then I think about the past and I wanna rip out my heart
Give it to someone who deserves it, in hopes for a new start
It's ironic I seek oneness, but seem to drift
a-part
I wanna be savior so I cut off my horns
God hasn't noticed
And the Devil still mourns
If there's any way to save you it'll be through these words
I'll teach by example, but I still gotta learn
In the end we all get what we deserve
Of course every end is just a new beginning
As our consciousness shifts
Our thoughts continue spinning
Our perception will change and it can happen in this life
The way you live can mend
Or it can bring strife
You might fuck it up once but you'll get another chance
You still gotta live like today is your last
Yesterday I thought I'd die having a blast
Now I'm not so sure I won't be saving your ass
Of course it's not so different from saving my own
When I'm climbing a mountain I can feel my headstone
I throw my art in the ocean before I dip my toes
So I can be the drop of blood
That will paint a rose.

# Thu Struggle

Our life is a series of complex anomalies
Suspended between consumption and waste
Don't live like today is your last
Live- like yesterday was
So you are surprised and grateful to be here now
Don't just make every second count
Count the seconds between the breath you take
And the steps you've taken to make every second count
Then step back and count to ten
Breathe – believe – see – be
The world – our universe
It's you – it's me
Everything stretching from the horizon
Lines are drawn
Over the barriers
Limiting our minds
From riding brain waves
Rolling up to the shores
Where our mothers wait
To pick agates
Tumbled by the turmoil
Of our conscious conflict
That constant struggle
Between the sea and stone
In every artists heart
Who seeks to know
Why one is expected to create
To compensate for the existence we own
Or should I say borrow
From the divine imagination
Of the evolutionary race

# Matt Maki

Matt Maki studied at Northern Michigan University and the University of Alabama; has served on the editorial boards of *Passages North*, *Black Warrior Review*, and *greatest lakes review*; founded the Marquette Poets Circle; and currently lives in Kyiv, Ukraine.

## Seasonal

Sometimes
a blue sky
is blue blue clouds.
Bluster. All
these baring trees.
The ones that were
once people: how
do they feel
about this?
Can one ever get used
to brightening,
then shed?
Even repeated loss
is loss.


(This poem first appeared in *Dunes Review.*)

## Walking in the garden in the cool of the day

The sun prolongs its setting here.
I linger as my sundial skin burns.
Sky color slips into
lake fish, beach stones,
night creeping in lake-first.

I fish out my cell, hoping for
missed calls, and notice time
slide from 9:34 to 9:33.
Miracles don't go as far today,
But how to spend a stolen minute?
Every September the extra hour
as wasted as April's vanishing hour, usually lost in a bar.

I spend the minute wishing the minute will repeat again,
and again, on an endless loop.
This whole continuum model
is what I hate. Why go back
to change something, or leap
forward to learn something,
and return to where you started?
Drab and dangerous,
nearly forgotten, the lake
looks like the Civil War.
Grey matters.

Leaves upturned in hoary green
shimmer the wind updraft
from sand to sky and my
feet brace for hard impact
with those mountains of clouds.
I want to take a perfect moment,
or a particularly pleasant year—
when everyone was alive
who needed to be, when
whatever you were doing you
at least enjoyed and did well
and found challenging enough,
and all you needed from the past
was to know it was over
and of the future
that it wouldn't be very bad

—and just keep repeating it.

But that pleasant year isn't coming back, especially since
the miraculous repeating minute
was three minutes ago.

It is getting cold.
I don't brush off my feet,
just shove them sandy
into socks and those into shoes,
like I'm an oyster and can make
something beautiful
out of something uncomfortable.

Across the bay, traffic flickers
on, same dead hue as sand,
the wooden steps rising
from these dunes but faded
even as they release their
last pinch of cedar.
On this side of grey-tinctured
windshield is a song *Grey*:
"The sky is grey, and the sand
is grey, and the ocean is grey."
Beyond it is grey light around
grey stones of grey church
supporting grey birds who,
on their flight to the grey lake,
pass over a dock brilliantly rusted.

(This poem first appeared, as a different version, in *Dunes Review*.)

# How to Use a Map

Unfold the map carefully so as not to tear its panicked embrace of itself. Gently lay it on the table, face up. Do not spend time examining the non-face's anatomy as the map is bashful, much like you were when you undressed in front of your first lover. Simply lay it on the kitchen table. Now a world of possibilities is in front of you.

Smooth the map with your hand. Flatten every wrinkle. Use a barely-warm iron to make it forget it was ever wrinkled. Defy Columbus. Keep rubbing it until it begins to polish. Make it shine. Purify the planet. Reflect heaven against itself.

Cover it with plastic soldiers, pewter canons. Play *Risk*. Be Napoleon. Be Hitler, Trump, Putin. Pick your scapegoat. Make the oceans red.

Walk around the table so many times that you can't remember which side of the map you're on. Fingerstab the map. Open your eyes and examine where your finger is standing. Buy a plane ticket there. Repeat the procedure to find a new location. Bring up the name of this place in every conversation for three days. Repeat procedure. Send a postcard to the government leader of that place.

Write the great American novel in tiny shorthand starting in the lower-right corner and ending in the upper left. Sell it to Random House. Idealistically refuse to sell the movie and merchandise rights for exactly eighteen months.

Lick a green spot on the map and explain what it tastes like—try to capture that flavor in a casserole. Scratch and sniff a yellow spot—design a perfume and twinned cologne that embody the essence of that smell. Use very little alcohol. Alternatively, make one unisex scent.

Say it is all a waste. Bargain with a man in the Middle East. Tip him off to your plans. Dump a glass of water over the map. Make it interesting—pour sweet tea with lots of ice cubes.

Lay a fish on it. Wrap it up. Call the map swaddling clothes and the fish your baby. Ask people if they think you have a pretty baby. Could it make it onto a Gerber jar? Or sell it on a street corner with baguettes. Or mail it to someone. Don't send it to your girlfriend. Send it to your ex-girlfriend. Send it to your mother in May, unless she has read Faulkner.

Practice your origami. Fold it into a box. Unfold it partially and make a frog. They are actually quite similar. Unfold it and make a swan. Have it swim in its own oceans.

Lay down on top of the map. Curl it around you like covers. Dream in it. Wet dream in it. Invite someone in with you and spill your mutual love over the world. Imagine all the people witnessing the act. Now, isn't that better?

(This poem first appeared in *Mid-American Review*.)

## Evidence

calicoed current
herringboned rocks
where brown was-moss
is moss again, grows
not only itself, but a tree,
paper antler
with twenty-nine eyes
and gills breathing in
green on green on up.
Beneath canopy more canopy
more green on green—
scaly limbs
replanting their tips
in noonblack ooze
of something
becoming everything
perhaps frond-canopy
for sand birthing silt
in drowsy cursive carvings
shaping ripples of current
over cement cum steel cum PVC pipe,
one jagged elbow snagging
discarded cloth
Beneath canopy more canopy.


(This poem was an honorable mention in the *Putting the Wild into Words*
poetry contest and anthology.)

## Sweden Day

The telephone startles him though he's still
awake, confused by morning shadows come
erotic, interrupted by her hushed

"Hello? Oh, hi. Nothing, no, nothing. No.
That thing. Later, okay? Yeah. Bye."
It's obviously him, the guy that he's

replacing, alpha wolf sniffing his bitch
for signs of beta. He doesn't ask.
She struggles out of bed, but he remains

in bed imagining a snowy field,
dawn in Sweden, wolves, circling, fangs unsheathed,
and snow drenched red with blood reeking copper.

A hollow thud awakens him and jerks
him to the bathroom where she's kneeling down.
He pulls her up and notices a gash

quite deep and newly-carved above her brow
with pennies glistening and spilling from
the wound, filling the tub around her feet.


(This poem first appeared in *Dunes Review*.)

# Gala Malherbe

Gala grew up in Munising, a small town on the shore of Lake Superior in the Upper Peninsula of Michigan. Her parents fostered her love of nature, introducing her and her two sisters to forests and trails with countless camping trips and hikes in Pictured Rocks National Lakeshore and Hiawatha National Forest. Her connection to nature grew with her, eventually prompting her to become an avid trail runner and nordic skier. Currently residing in Marquette, Michigan with her husband and three children, she is employed as a home health physical therapist where she travels Marquette County to serve homebound clients. She continues to spend much of her time outside, grateful for the chance to share the trails and lakeshore with her children. She has always found solace in writing, and the concise expression and mystery of poetry has attracted her since high school. She found her way to the Marquette Poets Circle in 2015 and has enjoyed challenging herself to grow as a writer and sharing the art of poetry with the group. She believes that poetry exists in every moment, if one is open to seeing it. Her chapbook, *Paper Words*, was published in 2017.

# A sunflower reflects

on her youth—how she crept unnoticed
from sleeping soil, fragile green sprout unraveling,
thready pale roots traveling
beyond oval safe seed shell,
intent to become

more. Each second, in increments,
cell upon cell stacked to perfection,
a beanstalk rising, reaching, higher,
erupting patiently—sun yellow
vibrance, a face, a beginning,

a story—how daily she swayed, engaged,
a loose embrace with summer breezes,
unfettered by scavengers, scarcity, storms,
head bobbing in praise song rhythm,
the deep green of her leaves
pumping with infinite
vitality.  A sun

flower reflects and stiffly sways,
color drained, brittle.  Head hangs
heavy.  Sallow goldfinches gather seeds
dropped like tears.  Cloaked in a dusk
of deepening gray, she bows
then winks as if to say, spring
will come again.

## Still Home

The painting leans crooked
against the wall,
first in a stack waiting
to be hung
in her new room.

Brush strokes capture
late season, leaves grown golden,
inevitable change.
Distant field grasses sway
green, still,
a wispy nest embracing
one small familiar house
that naps deserted
beneath an endless sky.

A suitcase waits open on the bed,
clothes folded neatly inside…
each day packed
and repacked.

She writes in labored loops and lines,
*This is a nice place.*
A nice place, but no place
like home.

She navigates through moments
beckoned by some flickering hope,
a porch light of sorts, left on
just for her.

*My daughter is coming to take
me home today. I won't be
here much longer. My mother,
she must be so worried about me.*

She has put on her coat.
Her purse rests in her lap.
The painting leans crooked
against the wall,
still home.

(This poem first appeared in *Paper Words*, 2017.)

## Leaving

His legacy leaks
from photos and keepsakes
that crowd dusty walls and end tables…
souvenirs, cookbooks, junk drawers, jewelry—
artifacts of one human story.

Bookshelves cradle collections,
fingerprints of preferences,
unique whorls of passions, pleasures,
pastimes, projects…

Braided rugs and faded afghans
steep in a potpourri of perfume,
spices, fabric softener, aftershave,
the aroma wrapping indefinitely around
the shoulders of the room, having
seeped deep into the upholstery
like episodic memories.

He rocks slowly,
reflecting on days and decades,
the wonders and wisdom of a lifetime
tucked away in daydreams,
like ticket stubs
in the pages of a journal.

His obituary rests on the table
next to newspapers, pizza coupons, bills…
printed in his own slanted script
on a yellow legal pad with curled corners,
waiting for its turn.

(This poem first appeared in *Paper Words*, 2017.)

# March

icicles hang
like steel bars
crowding her view
of the snow

that blinds her senses
and mocks her
as it mimics

the blank palate
of her mind
where fuzzy images
and ruptured patterns
march

like the icicles and
drip drip drip
like the droplets
that slowly slide
and harden around
her only window
to herself.


(This poem first appeared in *Paper Words*, 2017.)

## Junco

For me, it is the junco
though common,
that repeatedly surprises me
into rapt delight.
What if I lived as soft and light,
as busy and quick,
a perfect milk stain upon my belly,
an Easter egg dipped by tiny hands,
set free to be
whatever I am meant to be—
a joy, a message, a flicker of white,
a gift, a pause,
a poem in flight.


(This poem first appeared in *Paper Words*, 2017.)

# Beverly Matherne

Beverly Matherne's sixth bilingual work, *Bayou des Acadiens / Blind River*, a collection of short stories and prose poems, is from Éditions Perce-Neige, 2015. She has done over 300 readings across the U.S., Canada, and France, and in Wales, Belgium, Germany, and Spain. Invitations have taken her to Tulane University, Cornell University, Shakespeare and Company in Paris, and the United Nations in New York. She is one of eight authors, including Samuel Beckett and Vladimir Nabokov, whose bilingual writing process is the subject of a completed doctoral dissertation from the University of Paris III. Widely published, she has received seven first-place prizes, including the Hackney Literary Award for Poetry, and four Pushcart nominations. Professor Emerita of English at Northern Michigan University, she served as director of the MFA program in creative writing, director of the Visiting Writers Series, and poetry editor of *Passages North* literary magazine.

## Paper Boat

As though we'd rehearsed it . . .
our hands on the hairline of your forehead,
the tips of your shoulders,
your shins, ankles, the tops of your feet . . .
With one ceremonial push,
we launched you out the window,
through the fog in the swamp,
under the hidden moon.
We urged you on, did not oppose
the drift, as your breaths became
labored and fewer then stopped.
We let go of you,
the way a small boy floats a paper boat
in his back yard coulee,
the space between the boat and him widening.

(From Beverly Metherne's *La Grande Pointe*, Cross-Cultural Communications, 1995.)

## Feux Follets

By March, the Japanese tulips were bare,
their lilac petals on the ground so soft she lay upon them,
naked, her body opulent, the sky clear overhead.

No one in town knew anything about it – how
her hair came undone, her hair black and luminous
in the sun, her hair, its waves, folds of a funeral dress
spread on the still cool ground.

No one in town knew anything about it – her body
smooth, her body moist, beneath soil, her fingers
lengthening, circling shard and root.

No one knew anything about it – the tide coming
in, the tide going out, breaths of her body, the pull
from earth to moon, breaths of her body, votives,
in the holy night.

(This poem first appeared in *Runes: A Review of Poetry*, 2001.)

## Sons

When Junior came back from Spain in 66
at Christmas and didn't get killed in Vietnam,
Daddy cooked jambalaya and red beans
and invited the whole town to celebrate.

As the band played "Blueberry Hill,"
and Dixie Beer and mistletoe hung in the air,
June whisked me to the dance floor,
said how pretty and smart I was.
I drank his words, like everyone else,
wanted to know all about Spain, bullfights,
and long legs under red flamenco skirts.

Outside, firecrackers sparked
and shot, cherry bombs exploded,
cars blew their horns, bumper to bumper,
the levee blazed with bonfires,
all the way to New Orleans.

After midnight Mass, Mama
filled our bowls with andouille gumbo.
June headed home on a country lane.
His high school friend whizzed
skunk drunk in the other direction,
he didn't see June coming.
The sheriff broke the news.
Nobody cared for hot gumbo,
candied yams, or pralines.

The day after Christmas, mourners came.
We drank black coffee and stayed up
with June's body through the night.
Ernie Boy—just learning to play pitch and catch
with June—cried, threw up, and finally fell asleep
among the other little ones at the foot of the coffin.
My sister Shirley and I knelt beside it and prayed,
whispered about the smell of death,
and wondered whether everybody smelled it
but dared not say.

The next day, the pallbearers slid
the coffin in the mausoleum,
the way you slide a pan of bread into an oven.
The rain was cold and damp
and drenched the scarlet ribbons
on the great sprays of red roses at the wall.

That spring, Mama devoted herself to sorrow,
the way she did the stations of the cross
during Lent.  She started checking out books
on death and suffering, wore black,
put sorrow in June's buggy, tucked his
quilt at its neck, and pushed the buggy
out of her bedroom, through the kitchen,
down back steps, through cane fields,
and pastures, into swamp waters,
among wild orange irises.

She dredged the buggy from the swamp,
pushed it back to the house, down the driveway,
onto Grand Point Lane, to River Road,
to St. Joseph's Church.  She heaved,
she sweated, the wrinkles in her face stood taut.
She pulled the buggy up the church steps,
to the thick oak portal, up the aisle, to the altar,
did not genuflect, stared God straight in the eye,
and said "*Maudit fils de putain!*
You son of a bitch!"

The congregation froze, she turned
and waved her arms wildly,
"*Au diable avec tous de vous autres!*
To hell with all of you!"  She banged
The buggy down the altar steps,
down the aisle to the *Pietà*,
who held the dead Christ in her arms;
in her supplicating hand,
a crystal rosary fractured swords
of light from the rose window above.

"*Toi, toi. . . .* you, you. . . ." Her voiced cracked.
She hurled her arms around the neck
of the sorrowful mother, sobbed and sobbed,
crumpled, as if suddenly shot.

142

Daddy ran to her, gathered her in his arms.
"It's OK, Mama.  Let's go home, Mama."
Ten years later, melanoma tumors
covered Ernie Boy's body, and
Mama got restless again.

She got that wild look in her eyes
and searched closets, barns, and fields.
"What are you looking for?" asked Daddy.
"*Le maudit boghei de bébé!*
That goddamned buggy!" she said.

(This poem first appeared in Beverly Matherne's *Je Me Souviens de La Louisiane / I Remember Louisiana*, from March Street Press: Greensboro, NC, 1994.  It won the Grand Prize in the Superior Images Literary Competition sponsored by *The Mining Journal*, Marquette, Michigan, in 1994.)

## Holy Cross Cemetery

In
the
evening
at Holy
Cross Cemetery,
she stops dead in her tracks.  From snow
sameness emerges a white doe, rare as unicorn
in a southern French cloister.  Bare
maples send out sap.
Her lost son
finds his
way
home.

(This poem was first published in *Runes: A Review of Poetry*, eds. CB Follett and Susan Terris (2004):108.

# Pink Geraniums

I remember the first time
I saw them, in December,
pink geraniums in her office window,
hot pink, the only color against
limestone, snow, and gray clouds.

The flowers grew all winter,
shameless of their opulent blooms,
their large, circular leaves,
the way they filled the window,
as if to say: "Take me, take me,
I'm yours."

In those long stretches at 10 below,
I would take the short cut from the library,
time my treks with her office hours,
stop at her open door,
throw a "Hello, how goes?"
and bow like an old coot
from the Old West.

In my Ford pickup, I took her to Scheu's Café,
to chamber concerts, auctions in
Council Grove, Emporia, where
Flint Hills swell and dip, where
farmers and their wives unload
Bavarian crystal, Lunt silver, antique
Steinways and head south.

In spring, when purple crocuses
pushed up from the snow, I took her
to my wheat farm, threw
a table cloth on the barn floor.
Her shivering under me, straw
mingled in her black hair, I kissed her
full on the lips, smelled her woman,
smelled tractor grease, the earth, and gave
her my mother's double row of diamonds.

Today, her long dead, and me 90
among white sheets in my hospital bed,
I seek pink geraniums, hot pink, the only
color against limestone, snow, and clouds.

(This poem first appeared in *Uncommonplace: An Anthology of Contemporary Louisiana Poets,* ed. Ann Bewster Dobie. Louisiana State University Press, 1998. The poem won the Hackney Literary Award for Poetry, a national competition, in 1994.)

# Thane Padilla

Thane Padilla regularly walks the acequias (canals) of human progress in wonder and caution. When cool winds carry the words to light la chispa (the spark), Thane must take to the page and write. Otherwise he is a painter and sculptor easily distracted by friends, music, and food.

Thane Padilla studied art at the University of New Mexico and was born in Santa Fe, New Mexico.

He currently works as an iron worker in Arizona.

## Torch

> …out of the miles
> of breathing fields suddenly
> a small white town…
>
> --Philip Levine

A wall of clouds conceal the sunrise
and the security guard hands me my wallet
moist with contents. I unearth plastic cards
a photo of a niece from Africa living in Spain
and recall the snow bank as my billfold
unfolds. I am discovering life on Mars
not red but Yellow Dog and I was the brunt
of a winter's joke, wearing steal toe boots
where cement is mixed in hollow vocal
chords of earth while chunks of ore are held
close together in a body pile being hauled away.
I am apprentice to skilled laborers'
sons and grandsons muscle setting the nickel-
colored stage. Desire returns me home
in this meditation chamber of my gold
Toyota Tacoma truck, to paint on canvases cold
and silent white as jack pines who smile
as an ironworker under blue skies
of high northern plains who lost his wallet
last winter with six dollars of nothing
not so green anymore and an identification
card hibernating inside. My tired eyes
and unshaven jaw, the look of a creature
wondering why is he here. There are few clues
from this unearthed vessel of myself
whose bristly grin on a photo ID offers
little more than I don't know.
My calloused hands becoming softer again
and nearly frost-bitten toes in steel toe boots
again as gold or copper, say nothing
and in my Tacoma, go home, wielding
this other torch through the night shift
of canvases burning jack pines down
to these elemental words.

## Space Travel

Interstate 17,
ascending from the desert valley
The Valley-- they say in Phoenix.
I sometimes steer my truck with fingers tips only
and a free hand moves about as if searching
for a CD in the dark.

The ironworker in me disintegrates back in Tempe
               ASU stadium
fresh black asphalt parking lot,
bougainvillea—magenta nebula
emerge like Faith dust
dropping petals on pavement,
the breezes march them
       en masse
           pink
                scattered.

I'm far from that reality
as I round the freeway bend,
far from hawks cruising by the iron
suspended from our red crane,
low flying airliners could almost touch
the top of its boom.

Blowing spring dust turns to snow.
I wish to look to the median
to see elk carcasses from weeks gone by,
two crows high and big like eagles
make circles in a gray sky.

Dead elk
one a pile of bones melting to earth,
the other—whose body is a tunnel
eaten hollow by birds—filled with
light from ass-end to ribs and neck.

The song of Mastodon,
my final transport for this dream state.
        Upper Peninsula-
I recall this same trek- I was returning  home from a shutdown,
        a paper mill
        Powerhouse
                        the mines.


## Gisela

This is the beginning; the cosmos takes an in-breath.
Crosses are carried through the streets of Texmico, mournful faces,
heavy in white dresses and cotton shirts—the people Gisela loved
as the human beings they are. The Catholic stole adorned
with La Virgen de Guadalupe who floats in a white background,
symbol of purity, draped over wooden crosses.
                                    And the exhale happens
now. Gisela Mota, mayor of Texmico, you served one day in office.
Candles burn for days, grandmothers' tears infused with smoke of
copal. Your journey to the other side, with lilies, photos, crosses,
candles, Jesus and Mother Mary are set out for you.

Two candles cover the bullet holes in the floor and tenderness
is shaped in the form of flowers where your body once lay,
beside the crib of your nephew. Five days later Gisela's mother,
Juana Ocampo, carries a large portrait photo of her daughter
like a shield for a heart torn, marching together, giving voice—
"Out with Graco! Ya Basta! Justicia ahora!"

A single Monarch butterfly at sunrise, a plume of light, golden
with empowerment, unfolds its wings for lost souls drifting overhead
as voices enunciate the beautiful fight of the people. Gisela inhales.
"Here I am," she says. "You will see me digging through the trash
for corruption."

My parents were with me the morning of my murder, my nephew's
bottle of milk blessed by first glow of sunlight. We celebrated the night
before, laughing with new dreams, dancing and telling stories.
A mandala of tortas, salsa, and drink on the table.
                                    And the exhale happens
now—Thousands of butterflies with brother sun, unsheathed
from the chrysalis. Light and dark coexist in shapes.

149

# Robert Polsin

Robert Polsin has been writing poetry and short stories for the majority of his 23 years. Thankfully, he has progressed past the angsty navel-gazing characteristic of much of his early body of work. He has been featured in the collection, *N: Poems and Stories Volume One*. Bob would like to encourage readers and authors everywhere to get involved in their local literary and poetry communities, as they are an enriching, constructive, and generally kind and not very intimidating bunch. He is certainly very grateful for his experience with the Marquette Poets Circle and Thu Beat and all the dope poets he's learned from thereby.

## Memory(al)

Dead men do tell tales.
Same, tales are told of them.
And even when the rest fails,
a man may remember a friend.

He was, to be perhaps reductive,
Holofernes with nobler intention,
who met a Judith less seductive,
but with no less compelling invention.
For he brought the West's honey and milk
to the vulnerable of the wrong place and time.
So as attitudes changed among the ilk,
he paid summarily for his crime.

They sent you an image: his demise.
Four-by-six inches you held in your fingers–
No body, no neck, but head, lifeless eyes.
It's no wonder, no wonder, the memory lingers.

And no wonder you told me again and again,
before inevitably your body you shed.
For when one remembers a friend,
so too, one is compelled to speak for the dead.

# Jack

Be like a Jack Pine:
all jacked up, gnarl-faced,
curlicued bark and bone.

It's tough out there.
It's tough out there now.
So don't worry you don't grow straight.

Though your skin be ragged
and your futures sealed up with pitch,
remember it took fire for you to be born.
                    And a crucible is coming.

Don't become the phoenix,
who rises, perfect plumage perennial,
always just the same. (no)

Be like a pine cone:
glued shut, bound up, only popped awake
after hot winds blew, cinders flew,
inferno grew, and remains:
                            you.

Crack the dirt and eat the ash,
burrow up through old limbs flame-lashed.
Send squat-bladed needles to drink the sky,
shoot roots, the earth to ply.

It's a new wood, first successional,
the riotous part of life's progressional.

You, the vanguard, come to reclaim –
No! – remake a forest not the same.
And spread your limbs, not phoenix wings,
to shelter the young, slow-growing, other things.

The part you play, it is essential.
Some day thick boughs will, reverential,
look back upon what you've done
and know it's by this they kiss the sun.

So be a pine, Jack.
Own your ugly,
build from broken,
and grow.

## D.C.

DC: the men wear buckles on their shoes;
the streets they walk are broad.
Their suits are all tailored and tie-knots taut,
man'cured as if by law.

Although the capitol gleams bloodless white,
I hear the house is red.
And in voices in rest'rants and porticos
will gossip what's ahead.

But not for me, not for me.
This place is not for me!
I cannot bear the pretension
and, by extension, the shackling of hearts free.

I feel so funny walking on the grass,
but comply, "yes, ma'am," to the guard
as I empty from my pockets
any item that is hard.

I say, "thank you," to the waiter
after, "I'll have the duck,"
and somehow yet feel envy
even as I eat my luck.

The city is magnificent, brilliant.
Yes, this I will admit.
As well, I must not lie to you, I do
quickly tire of its shit.

# Janeen Pergrin Rastall

Janeen Pergrin Rastall lives with her partner Richard J. Rastall in Gordon, MI (population 2). Janeen is the author of *In the Yellowed House* (dancing girl press, 2014), *Objects May Appear Closer (*Celery City Chapbooks, 2015). She is a co-author with Les Kay, Allie Marini and Sandra Marchetti of *Heart Radicals* (ELJ Publications, 2016, new and expanded edition, Black Magic Media, 2018). She co-authored the chapbooks, *Romancing The Geek* (2013) and *True Companions* (Gordon Publications, 2017) with Richard J. Rastall. Together they co-wrote the play *Romancing The Geek* which premiered in 2014. Her work has been nominated multiple times for a Best of the Net Award and for the Pushcart Prize. Her poetry has appeared in several publications including: *Border Crossing, The Raleigh Review, Prime Number Magazine, North Dakota Quarterly* and *The Fourth River*. She was the co-recipient with Richard J. Rastall of the City of Marquette Arts Culture Center's Community Arts Activist Award for 2017. Please visit her at her website: janeenpergrinrastall.wordpress.com

## Tend

What if you could propagate Time,
take a slip with pinking shears,
put it in a jelly jar?
What if you spill well water
until the stem drifts lazily, find a space
on the sill where the sun lolls
across Formica? What if you wait
through days, rinse cups,
scrape plates and stare
only at rust blooms
around the sink's strainer
until that shoot you love
grows tendrils? Strands thicken;
press the glass, and new minutes
with your mother pull towards the pane.

(This poem first appeared in *Objects May Appear Closer* (Celery City Chapbooks, 2015.))

# Photograph of Mom, Age 3, Sitting in the Pasture

On summer afternoons, my mother sits
on the stoop, a bowl of potatoes in her lap,
a pot beside her. She places the peeler
at the tip of a potato and unravels the skin.
A single dark curl winds away
from the moist white heart.

She can do it by feel, her eyes follow robins
in the maples, bumbles tasting clover
on the lawn. Worry sheds from her face,
she smiles like the girl in the photograph
on her father's mantelpiece.


(This poem first appeared in *Objects May Appear Closer* (Celery City Chapbooks, 2015.))

## Photograph of Mom in Angora Sweater, Arlington, OH, 1959

She left her Polish on the farm:
the stink of cabbage cooking,
work shirts drying on the line.
She gathered up a Bachelor's,
studied chemistry, read Millay,
wallpapered the colonial,
did decoupage, played croquet,
but sometimes she would wake,
her fist clenched
around a phantom weight—
feed-corn heavy in her hand,
the click of the furnace
like chickens scratching at the pan.


(This poem first appeared in *Objects May Appear Closer* (Celery City Chapbooks, 2015.))

# Imprinting

*You were aimed from birth.  - William Stafford*

Migration

For long hours
it is only roofs,
a backlit yard flickering
or a basketball net
reaching to snare the night.
Streets meet, cross,
thin to single threads.
Trees take over,
swell to canopies.
A pool has been calling since birth,
its coordinates tattooed on DNA.
Even though a road draws a loop around the shore,
houses perch on the water's lip,
the gander knows this lake,
lands feet first, calls to the flock,
beacons them home.


Racine

The town has collapsed in the center,
strip malls spreading north and south.
Once you see the tarnished Piggly Wiggly,
you know your way.
You follow the old bus route,
wind past the park and cemetery,
recreate the rides of summer:
your grandmother close beside you,
her purse between her feet,
in crimped hands, she holds a paper sack–
apples, Wonder Bread, a waxed envelope of lunchmeat.
You drive without hesitation
to the house on the cul-de-sac,
look for the window
where you pressed your nose against the glass
to watch your grandfather,
lunch pail in hand,
walk to the tannery.

158

Lakestruck

An accident led you here.
You went to see another frozen lake,
to walk among ice volcanoes,
listen to the floes bump and crack.
You did not know
Superior waited
deep-hearted,
battering its song
against black rocks.
You have been pulled in
like trout
from the Au Train,
or the Chocolay,
drawn to deeper waters.
Your breath syncs to the sound of the surf.


(This poem first appeared in *Heron Tree.*)

# Richard J. Rastall

Richard J. Rastall is married to the poet Janeen Pergrin Rastall. They live in Gordon, Michigan.

He has an undergraduate degree and a master degree in mathematics from Michigan State University. He graduated from the Thomas M. Cooley Law School and has a master degree in laws in taxation from New York University.

He has previously published the chap book, *Ice Volcanoes, 3ⁿᵈ Ed.,* (Gordon Publications, 2016), and with Janeen Pergrin Rastall, the chapbooks, *Romancing The Geek* (2013) and *True Companions* (Gordon Publications, 2017). He co-wrote with Janeen Pergrin Rastall the play *Romancing The Geek* which premiered in 2014.

He was the co-recipient with Janeen Pergrin Rastall of the City of Marquette Arts Culture Center's Community Arts Activist Award for 2017.

## Knowledge

Vision and light scream across the black flood,
and blow shadow's tongue away.

It is essential…

like the next moment,

like skin.


## PTSD

Grab the edge of Lake Superior and lift,
floating on the bottom are heavy memories,
hard to hold,
yet explosive like snap-dragons.

Touch one…
poke the remnants with a stick,
dig in your own ashes.


## Artifacts

For weeks I chisel my feelings for you out of my bones.
Some pieces are hot, some ash edged.

Spread on a table, like an impossible jig saw puzzle,
I hold the pieces, put them next to each other, search for connections.

In time, a form develops.

I hold it to the mirror.
Not what I expected.

My heart responds,
the form is absorbed.


(These poems appeared in *Ice Volcanoes*, 3rd Edition (Gordon Publications, 2016.))

## Schrodinger's Cat

Schrodinger's cat escaped.

It had had it…
being alive and dead at the same time.

An observer would need to measure some data to answer the question,
but the cat had no deal that it would be the gossip of paradox.

It remembered hearing someone say: "…think outside the box…".

It made sure that no one saw it escape.

And, unseen, it went to a deep part of the forest.

Thus, it was simultaneously in the box (alive and dead) and in the forest.

A tree fell in the forest.

Schrodinger's cat did not hear the tree before the tree crushed it…
…or did it?


(This poem appeared in *Ice Volcanoes*, 3rd Edition, (Gordon Publications, 2016.))

## The Tear Horizon

Is there a tear when I don't feel it?
When I don't see it?

Is a tear,
like the universe,
with quarks and mesons,
behaving like pixels on a video game screen,
apparently whole but with more holes than not.

Each game room and level off screen,
as the universe beyond the limit of our senses,

having fun existentially as particles and waves,
until they cross our event horizon,

to become deterministic…

puppets on strings,

forced to follow the puppeteer's rules…

as the pixels on my screen,
the subatomic particles within my senses,

and the critical mass of loss in a tear,

a tear not felt until the next sorrow.

(This poem appeared in *Ice Volcanoes*, 3rd Edition (Gordon Publications, 2016))

# Helen Haskell Remien

Helen Haskell Remien lives in Ishpeming, Michigan where she and her husband Cam raised their two sons. She received her MA in creative writing from Northern Michigan University and has published a chapbook of poems, *Diving Down*, a full-length manuscript of poetry, *Wild Ground*, a memoir, *Ebb & Flow*, and has a forthcoming book of essays, *I'm Not Too Much For Me!!!*, expected to be out later in 2017. Presently, she teaches yoga, creativity workshops, and is proprietor of Joy Center, a sanctuary for body/mind/spirit. Helen delights in her daily writing practices, her romps in the wilds of nature, and her travels far and near.

## I Believe

I believe in waves
waves of breath
waves of hair
hand waves, double waves
two palms up
I believe in abundance
an earth overflowing
I believe in honey bees
sweet nectar, the buzz of wings

I believe in the human heart
in life lived with heart
thrumming in youth and elders
I believe in fairies
in elves, in mischief
I believe that happiness dwells within us
that we can draw on its waters
whenever we want
I believe in clear waters

I believe in bubbles, pink, glistening
drawn from a wand
I believe in sturdy feet
in rich black dirt
red iron ore dirt
sand pounder fine by waves
waves of light
waves of water
waves crashing on the shore

## Hips Sing the Blues

A seediness in these hips
blue haze in the room
and I am on the threshold-
a Bette Davis bitch in these hips
funeral march and springtime birth
these hips are not a clean poem
prissy little list
these hips are an ocean saying
sing the whole song

## When the Rain Comes

I will strip down to bare feet and bare bones
leaves will spring full-force into summer
lilacs will bloom sweet fragrance into the air
lakes will fill and droplets spiral in whirls and twirls
lilies of the valley will dance with late-blooming iris
and the iris will say I'm feeling wild today!
When the rains come the seeds will swell
flourish is a word that will fall easily from my tongue
I will run naked through grass honoring my body
I will be Mother Nature cradling ripened eggs in my hands
I will be young again
when the rains come

# I'm Hungry

I'm hungry for ripe tomatoes warm juicy thick-sliced
for olives and olive oil and coarse salt
I'm hungry for basil's soft under-leaves
for bread full-grained hand-kneeded fresh-baked
I'm hungry for warm sun on a spacious day
for the tart bite of lime and cold fizzling water
I'm hungry for smooth rock and waves lapping
for the depths to rock the boat
I'm hungry and there is a white feather
tucked in the crack of stone
there is a smooth  pool now gently wind-rippled
I'm hungry for you to brush my still surface
for a ripple of pleasure to light my waters

## La Dolce Vita
Cinque Terre, Italy

You know, as you hike high above the town
into the mountains, as you stop and cup the bursting
grapes, as you taste the sweet stickiness of a ripe fig,
as you hear the peaches groan, that Bacchus himself
must have felt it, too, this deep something
that is in the soil and in the olive branches and in their
olive skin and in the juice of the olive drenched
through this slice of focaccia you are now eating
an hour later in a secluded cove where the sirens sing.
Is it the flickering silver of the schools of anchovy,
the mullet fish flying high in synchrony toward the
shore that bring a secret joy to an Italian siren?
The opera in the Cinque is in the air,
in the hazelnut gelato that is smooth and creamy,
as nourishing to the soul as if you are sucking heaven
from the cow's udder itself and how, how do you allow
it in, all this secret joy, this cry that says,
Live it! Live it!
Don't handle it. Don't stuff it in your hiking boots,
into khaki quick-dry pants. Rip off those layers
of containment, drink it in, get drunk with it all
and, when the sun sets, sit outside on the break-wall
and watch the pink and golden lights
ripple across the sea.


(This poem first appeared in *Wild Ground*.)

169

# Bert Riesterer

From Philosophy to Poetry.

Bert, a Detroit boy, was born in 1935 the only child of German immigrant parents who fostered an interest in nature and learning. His education, both basic and higher (Wayne State University B.A. M.A. Ph.D), were mainly in Detroit. Thanks to a German relative, his senior college year was spent in Germany, where he was introduced at the famous and prestigious University of Heidelberg to several of the major German thinkers in the second half of the twentieth century. This experience resulted in a shift from a general European history major to continental philosophy which, as a graduate student, he pursued and later taught under the flexible heading of European Intellectual History. His teaching career began at Wayne State, moved to Albion College, and settled at the Indianapolis campus of Indiana University. Shortly after retiring in 1999 and moving from the city to the hard woods and soft hills of South Central Indiana, he began working on a brief philosophical memoir and, at the encouragement of wife and daughters, tried his hand at poetry. The philosophical memoir: *Seeking Meaning, from Words To The Wordless* was finally self-published (first edition 2009, second in 2015). His poetry book: *Paths To The Page* (first edition 2012, improved version 2016), also self-published, encompasses his sojourn in the Indiana woods as well as the move to the Upper Peninsula of Michigan in 2007. The awe inspiring experience of the raw untamed nature of large stretches of the Lake Superior shore and the surrounding woods was truly transformative for him, the culmination of a lifelong spiritual journey from philosophy to poetry.

# Hunger

It grumbles and roars
claws the rocks
then glistens them
with a quick lick
before the claws retract
and the pads slap the sand
raising hundreds of tiny bubbles.

When ravenous
it ignores the rocks and sand
biting savagely into the hefty shore itself.
Gaping holes with tattered edges
expose thickly packed slices of
red sandstone that decay to a
meager but surprisingly
nourishing crust.

Appetite stilled
it smacks its lips and
swishes thin sheets of saliva
into these ragged openings
a rinse their porous bottoms
absorb almost instantly.

Others
equally hungry
but for a different fare
also come here to feed.

It's where
my first granddaughter
was baptized.


(This poem first appeared in *Paths to the Page,* 2012, 2016.)

## Leaves

When it comes to trees
most admire trunk and limbs.
I go for the leaves.

Lose them to moths and beetles,
the mighty frame notwithstanding,
serious damage has been done.

A few can with difficulty make a new set
but never as lush and vigorous.
Most simply die.

It's not the dark and heavy pith of things
so arduously extracted by philosophers
and scientists.

It's what is joyously put forth
numberless insatiable ephemeral
to revel in the light.


(This poem first appeared in *Paths to the Page,* 2012, 2016.)

# Donnelly Widerness Preserve
(Upper Peninsula)

Nestled in a huge gorge
the river peacefully uncoils its way
to the distant Lake.

Intermittent sunshine casts
a dazzling gleam on select stretches.

Stone based wavelets mimic
the twists of wary trout.

High above its broad banks
I wander the tree rich trail.
Ancient hemlocks, spruce, pine
and cedar reign majestically
unabashed by the occasional
challenge of feisty young saplings.

Total quiet

Blessed Peace

The soul supplants the self

Boundaries fade

The rarity of Oneness.


(This poem first appeared in *Paths to the Page,* 2012, 2016.)

## Altars

Not all are in churches.
You can also find them
along the shores of Lake Superior.

There on windy days the waves
piously roar spittle tinged amens
as they genuflect with a hefty plunge-thump
before the stone platforms
that jut out from the cliffs.

Sometimes they get so carried away
by the frenzy of worship
that they splatter themselves
across the surface of the stone
completely shattering the decorum
that we are taught befits
the seriousness of true worship.

Yet their God is not at all
displeased, indeed just the opposite.
He revels in their exuberance and even
incites them to greater ecstatic excess.

For me the scene is irresistible.
I can't keep myself from mounting the altar
and kneeling before the worshippers arms spread wide
roaring and screaming with them
as they drench my body and ignite my soul.


(This poem first appeared in *Paths to the Page*, 2012, 2016.)

## Marquette 200
(Annual Sled Dog Race)

Before I could see them I heard them. At first distant barking yapping and howling. Then when I arrived an entire symphony. Every possible sound that they can make was present at full volume. It went straight to the core. My heart was thumping and my body quivering with excitement. The wild guys were here and raring to run. Wild? They've been domesticated, disciplined, and trained for millennia. True. But these husky, malamute, siberian, and other mixed breeds were so worked up, yowling and lunging against their traces, that more than mere dog was at hand. Their lupine ancestors were shining through their eyes and coursing in their blood.

After a long and disappointing scholarly career I came to Michigan's Upper Peninsula seeking what was left of wilderness. Here I found some of it in teams of twelve pulling a sled. Again I shuddered with pleasure too moved to speak, and kept my head down so the others wouldn't see my tears. Dear God before I go let me ride, however briefly, on such a sled.

Horses are large elegant marvelous animals. When they run it's sheer beauty. But for me it's this raucous unruly mob, disciplined and harnessed into a unified driving force, singing their raw song of primeval joy. It reawakens the primitive in me, the awestruck ice age Cro-Magnon who neither Ph.D. nor thirty years of academia has eradicated, the irresistible call of the wild.

(This poem first appeared in *Paths to the Page,* 2012, 2016.)

# Omari Rouse

Omari "O.J." Rouse is a Detroit, MI native who settled in the Upper Peninsula of Michigan in 2011. Always having a love of writing since a young age, Omari tried his hand at lyric writing at the age of 14 aspiring to be the next big rapper. After years of honing his craft, expanding his vocabulary and literary horizons, and with minimal success in being a breakout rap star; opportunity came when an open mic competition was held in the settlement town of Houghton, MI. He entered this competition not to win, but to make a lasting impact and re-invent himself. At the end of a brief introduction, Omari said a phrase that gave firm reasoning behind his recent change: Not all messages need a melody. With that he delivered his first poem, *Death of an Unborn Lyricist,* to great praise and appreciation. Today, traces of lyricism and wordplay can be found in his writings, showcasing that his over 15 years of practice, talent, and creativity have not gone to waste.

## Black River

I can see the glow from afar
Teasing one another throughout the day
Inching ever closer to embrace, engulf in tender passion
Rippling waves are reminiscent of silky sands through gentle blowing winds
A kiss is shared at the horizon
Deeper…deeper…deeper into each other they go
Sun and sea; sweet lovers that meet nightly
Cherishing each moment going into the night, until they part ways in the morning
The Black River
Where the sun and sea meet at dusk
Shamelessly displaying their enchanting beauty for all to take in.

# PRODUCT OF MY ENVIRONMENT

Take one male and one female add love and passion, a child is born.

## I'M A PRODUCT OF MY ENVIRONMENT

Integrate African culture, hip hop influence, and urban ghettos.
Stereotypes run rampant; yet hold some truth to who we are supposed to be.
Subtract common sense; add pride for learned mannerisms that is looked upon as a social negative.
The number of closed down schools plus lack of alternative curricular activities is proportional to the level of crime that occurs; what's the difference?

## I'M A PRODUCT OF MY ENVIRONMENT.

Stupidity is equal to lack of knowledge plus ignorance of self.
Those who want us to learn about ourselves don't fully teach us who we really are.
History has been distorted, facts subtracted from the books, false flash and glamour integrated into our minds.
How can you tell us that we can be anything yet don't tell us everything?
Because you tell us what YOU want us to be corporate exec.
YOU give out the problem, but offer no solution. When we solve the problem, you say that it's wrong.
THEN LAUGH.

## I'M A PRODUCT OF MY ENVIRONMENT.

As crime multiplies, divisions between loyalty and duty grow, leaving only a small remainder of police protection within a certain margin.
Subtract love, hope, care, and respect; add guns, drugs, corruption, and desperation.
That's a formula for a dying city.
No law, no love, no life, no reason to live.
Welcome to Urban City, USA, population: too many.

## I'M A PRODUCT OF MY ENVIRONMENT.

Shimmers of hope lose continuity.
A positive person is less than a negative group of people.
But wait, that's not a true statement. Yes, one is less than two, that's true.
Yet, Gandhi was positive, Martin Luther King was positive, Mother Theresa was positive, Jesus Christ was positive. A single person can make a powerful impact.
A positive person is less than a negative group of people. How is this not a true statement?
It's simple mathematics.

178

A POSITIVE ONE IS ALWAYS GREATER THAN A NEGATIVE ANYTHING.
Society, life, our environment, even ourselves can always bring us down.
But they are the same things that can drive us to be our best

**I'M A PRODUCT OF MY ENVIRONMENT.**

## Frozen Ballet

Graceful. Elegant. Beautiful. Unique.
All words to describe you in the slightest detail
I see many like you, but none exactly as you are
Dancing to your own melody through the wafting breeze
Where are you going beautiful one?
Are you coming to me? Am I the chosen one of your sweet touch?
Gliding over me ever so gently, I await you
Fall to me
I open up to you
Let me embrace you
I wish to swallow the very essence of your evanescent nourishment
Left to right, back and forth, to and fro, ever closer
Land on my tongue, little snowflake
Send me to the sweet nirvana within the bitter cold
Melt away for now, but there are others to come and take your place

# Wolf In Human's Clothing

I walk alone, ever traveling a maze of naturally changing walls
There are others like me…were like me.
Were they like me?
Only in look, I suppose, portraying only a façade of standing in unity
We blended as a scene of camouflage for protection, yet we couldn't see eye to eye
They did not have the same vision as I did
They didn't notice how the hunters became the hunted
I move alone, separate from the analogous pack
In a forest of metal, concrete, and false wood structure, I am a lone wolf

## Shut Up and Enjoy the Flowers

Roses are red, violets are blue
Some other stuff happened, but I'm not yet through
It snows in July and mosquitoes do bite
On a good day, you can see a starry night
It's time to grow up, with the roses and violets
But for now, I give you silence…
So shut up and enjoy the flowers

# Christine Saari

Christine Saari, writer and visual artist, grew up on a farm in the foothills of the Austrian Alps. The formative years of her childhood during and after World War II are featured in her memoir "Love and War at Stag Farm. The story of Hirschengut, an Austrian Mountain Farm 1938 - 1948" (Published 2011).

In 1964 she immigrated to the United States. She lived with her American husband and two children in Boston, before moving to the Upper Peninsula of Michigan in 1971. There she worked as a freelance journalist, took up photography, and spent 20 years creating her mixed media project Family Album. This body of work is now installed in the Hayloft Gallery at the Austrian farm, where she spends three months a year.

Christine Saari is a member of the WOW (Women of Washington) Studio in Marquette, where she is working on an ongoing recycling series: Cigar Box Shrines.

Recently, Christine Saari began writing poetry. She has found the stimulation through the Marquette Poets Circle a great help in this endeavor. The 5 "garment" poems are part of a larger series of poems dedicated to fabric and garments for special occasions.

# The Baptismal Gown

She did not leave it behind,
the baptismal gown
stitched for my mother
in 1906: A cloud of white lace.

It came along,
when her dead husband's children
kicked her out and she left
to keep house for her brother.

She carried it to the Austrian Alps
for her granddaughter's baptism,
to link the generations,
to soothe fears of impending war.

The gown sailed to America
waiting for our son's christening.
In an alien church in Boston
my grandmother's gown felt like home.

Our grandson wore the lace gown
his great grandmother had sewn.
Four generations on two continents
were baptized in it:

In Protestant churches, in Catholic chapels,
in Pomerania by the Baltic Sea,
in the Austrian mountains, on the Atlantic coast
on the shores of Lake Superior:

Soon our grandson will marry.
His bride to be eyed the gown
hanging from a gallery beam
in Austria and smiled.

I see a child,
a child still a dream.
I see a small face peek
out of a cloud of white lace.

## My Wedding Dress

Delicate butterflies
woven into smooth brocade silk -
an elegant yet cheerful dress,
sewn in a Hong Kong tailor shop.

Hidden in an Asian trunk
on an Italian luxury liner
you journeyed
from Singapore to Genua,

At our wedding
in an Austrian village church
your butterflies danced
to the music of Mozart,

You sailed across the Atlantic to America
and hung in the closets of our houses.
One day I took you to the studio
and cut you up.

Your butterflies now adorn
boxes and shrines.
They have come out of the darkness
and twirl in the light,

# The Dowry

Gleaming white they swirl in the morning sun,
like gossamer, suspended
in the stillness of the gallery.

Camisoles and chemises,
drawers and petticoats,
diaphanous batiste from Switzerland.

Iridescent mother of pearl,
eyelet embroidery, lace,
finer than ice work on winter windows.

Ghosts from a time when women spent years
stitching their dowry underwear
only their husbands could see.

My grandmother's sister, Gisela Schwarz,
assembled these Victorian wonders of craftsmanship
only to die, mysteriously, on her honeymoon.

Her dowry waited, hidden in a flower-painted trunk,
not to be worn, until I became
the keeper of this family legacy,

The magic hands of my Austrian seamstress
made wasp-waisted camisoles
fit my body free of corsets.

They turned lace edged drawer pants
into petticoats and Dirndl sleeves,
sewed nightgowns into summer dresses.

I am too old now to don
fluffy garments of white lace.
My granddaughters have more practical tastes.

Gleaming white they swirl in the morning sun,
like gossamer, suspended
in the stillness of the gallery.

## Old Kimono

This is why Friedel married Max:
Not for love, but for adventure.
Exotic parcels arrived from Japan:
A lacquer box. An ivory fan.
A silk kimono.

The kimono traveled to America
and, never worn,
sat in my closet for 50 years.
Now moths have attacked
the old silk garment.

I open seams to save
the fabric's hand-painted landscapes,
embroidered miniature cranes,
delicate beauty
on black brocade.

Barely enough fabric is left
to make a scarf,
a scarf to preserve
a sliver of the past,
and to remember an old friend.

# The Nightgown

(Dedicated to Ileana Renfrew, in memory of Gladys)

The camison, our nightgown:
Lacy, diaphanous, embroidered.
The nightgown Gladys had bought
to please her lover.
The nightgown she had worn
when she conceived her son.
The nightgown she had given me
to birth my child.
*Not suitable for birthing,* she had said,
*but oh, so beautiful!*

*Don't come,* Gladys said,
when I called from Marquette to Uruguay.
*I am wearing our nightgown,*
*Don't come. You are already here.*

Two days later Gladys died.
She wore the nightgown she had treasured
for fifty years,
our camison that tied us
from one continent to another.

Weeks later a package arrived.
In it: The nightgown. Our camison.

# John Taylor

John Taylor is an author, artist, and activist based out of Marquette, Michigan. John was born in Caro, Michigan, in 1983 and has resided in Marquette county since 2007. John earned a certificate in creative writing from Stratford Career Institute, and is currently the editor of the newsletter for the Alger/Marquette affiliate of National Alliance on Mental Illness(NAMI). His Poetry, Fiction, and Essays have appeared in the *The Mythic Circle*, the *Marquette Monthly*, *The Dieselpunk e-Pulp Showcase Vol. 2*, and the *Northcare Network* quarterly newsletter. Additionally, John's illustrations have appeared in the *Abilene Reflector-Chronicle* (Abilene, Kansas) Newspaper, savethewildup.org and swordsandsorcerymagazine.com's websites, and in many local flyers and 'zines.

His artistic inspirations include H.P Lovecraft, William Blake, Edgar Allan Poe, Lewis Carroll, and H.R. Giger. John's works deal with dreamlike themes of the dark and fantastic.

He currently resides in north Marquette with his wife, Miriam.

# Teratophobia

She sees the dark museum hall, grisly are its sights
a gallery of jars filled with twisted flesh and bone
skulls with strange deformities, and pickled parasites
Give flight to anxieties she wished were left alone

*The smell of formaldehyde, the perfume of the damned...*

One exhibit beckons her ignored by passers by
A cute little skeleton, two bodies with one head
The museum's saddest story unfolds in her mind's eye
She feels for her womb, curiosity turns to dread

*The plaque reads: mono-cephalic conjoined twins, 1899.*

She hears the skeleton's lament, silently it cries
Had it known a mother's touch or parent's gentle hand?
She looks away and wonders, tears welling in her eyes
Had it known a crib beside the cold museum stand?

*Did it ever hear a lullaby?*

Sadness fills it's hollow eyes, its little rib-cage bare
A shudder wracks her body from head down to her womb
Eliciting from the crowds their cold, disgusted stare
Could her own child be destined for such a public tomb?

*Tell me that's not a kidney in the jar next to it...*

She weeps not for the skeleton, rather for herself
She'd feel no sorrow for its fate or wish it wasn't dead
If it was her own child displayed, on that museum shelf
She cannot bring herself to love two bodies and one head

*Teratophobia (noun): an abnormal fear of giving birth to a monster....*

Her baby's kicks within her womb, stir her troubled mind
Now overcome with visions of her deformed child's screams
She flees the frightful scene, leaves the skeleton behind
The nightmare stands triumphant atop her shattered dreams

*Is that book bound in human flesh? I'm going to be sick!*

189

Past rows of distorted glass, preserved eyes and livers
Morbid displays proclaiming that life is never fair
She exits the macabre hall, and all it's shivers
At last give way to a world of precious sunlit air

*"Strange and informative!" the brochure said...*

Silently, she counts the days until the baby's date
She weeps not for the decision that she's about make
Surely, that museum will not be her her child's fate
She knows the little skeleton has no heart to break

*No, Doctor, I don't want to see the scan results...*

# The Legend of the Wild Man

The bazaar of Babylon fell silent as he stepped into the square,
an ancient time-worn hunter, wild eyed and gray of hair.
Barefoot with a wooden spear, clothed in skins of beasts,
His features dark and savage, as in the lands northeast.
The merchant people whispered tales of men from long ago,
who dwelt in caves and savage things did hunt with club and bow.

Throwback! Barbarian!
Gray of hair and face.
This lone wild man remains
of a lost and bygone race.

He spoke no word, the Wild Man, nor uttered any sound,
but took his ancient wooden spear and etched into the ground;
a portrait of a horrid thing, a dragon without wings,
feasted on great warriors, its gut the tomb of kings.
He pointed at the image of the beast from deepest Hell
and gestured curiosity of where the creature dwells.

Ignorant! Illiterate!
To believe a wild tale.
But then a traveler spoke a name
and his mockers all grew pale.

The Sirrush-cave of Belthshazar, the ancient throne of fear
where heathen lords once sacrificed a maiden twice a year,
unto fiends who fed on men like the image in the dust.
And on this traveler's account the Wild Man put his trust.
And ventured forth still westward, toward the nearby Sirrush-cave,
joined by those men of Babylon too bold to fear the grave.

Impossible! Incredible!
The Wild Man's quest did seem.
But was is but a moment ago,
he himself was but a dream.

They followed him for hours, up the grim and rocky path
strewn everywhere were bones of men, slain by primal wrath.
Through this barren rocky grave, a chill, fell wind now moans.
Its whispers name the unhallowed place; it is the Vale of Bones.
Ahead an altar black and grim, forged in an elder age,
bore upon it the bloodstains of a great and elder rage.

Unsettling! Unnerving!
The dead among the stones.
But even not so dreadful as
the cave above the bones.

The Sirrush-cave of Belthshazar silenced them in awe.
That graven arch and elder runes that formed a fearsome maw.
Surely greater hands than men's had hewn such giant stones,
and surely far more vile jaws had filled the Vale of Bones.
The Wild Man then charged ahead and on the altar stood
and with his elder spear in hand, revealed a flute of wood.

Enchanting! Enticing!
His melody fills the air
now answered by a hellish roar
within the fearsome lair.

The beast broke forth, a scaly fiend, upon two legs like towers.
Thick of hide and bony snout, its hunger was its power
With flailing tail and raging jaws ready to devour.
The Wild Man, last of his kind, faced his finest hour.
Approaching now before him through the graven ring,
was the dreadful shadow of the Tyrant Lizard's king.

Saurian! Reptilian!
Dread fiend of bygone age!
Dark lord of the carnivores,
Ravenous with rage!

The Wild Man, he trembled not, nor showed the slightest fear,
but uttered forth a battle cry and raised his honored spear.
He struck like lightning, drew first blood, the Tyrant roared in pain,
and the awestruck Men of Babylon knew his quest was not in vain.
But the Tyrant knew no fear that day, upon the Vale of Bones,
and lashed out with fearsome talons to forge wounds of its own.

Brutality! Savagery!
Man and beast trade blows.
Feral strength and primal wrath
Consume the ancient foes.

The Wild Man was fearless still, thought cut by jagged snout,
gave no quarter, not an inch, in this his final bout.
Both alone, both the last, vanished are their kind.
But for the glory of the hunt, he'd end his rival's line.
The elder world, and savage times, would be at last laid low.
And for the honor of his tribe, he'd strike the final blow.

Valor! Honor!
His courage paves the way
to glory now and evermore,
smite the beast, seize the day!

For bloody hours the battle raged, until the light began to fail
When in despair , the Wild Man charged and seized its scaly tail.
Across its back he ran and leapt, with feral hunter's skill.
And with his spear he rent its throat, behold the epic kill!
With a final raging cry, the blow of death found home,
And the Tyrant's ruin was writ in blood upon the Vale of Bones.

Triumphant! Magnificent!
The Wild Man prevails.
His savage bane lies cold and dead,
by mighty spear impaled.

Triumphant, torn, and ragged, his nightmare foe now past.
His quest fulfilled, his life complete, the Wild Man breathes his last.
The Men of Babylon stood in awe of their hero slain
And took a vow upon his grave that he had not died in vain.
To ever live with courage, and right what wrongs they can
And fight with honor to the end, as did the Wild Man.

Destiny! Integrity!
The Men of Babylon
swore with their dying breath
to ever carry on.

For the Wild Man weep not, be not distressed nor scared.
For by tales of his courage, fair Andromeda was spared.
For him Saint George fought dragons, and Arthur's men were brave.
For knighthood was born of an oath, upon the Wild Man's grave.

(First appeared in *Mythic Circle*, Vol.36 in 2014,)

# Hail Great Queen

All hail Queen great and terrible, of rancorous damnation!
Usurper of Liberty's crown, the glorious damnation!

She towers over mountains high, cruel titan cast in jade
Avatar of darkest desires, of sensuous damnation

How beautiful the feet of her that lay waste the promised land!
Who's every footstep leaves a grave of sulfurous damnation

*"Ave, Magna Regina et treminadae majestis!"*

Heroes seem as ants, saints in the hands of an angry goddess
The power of swords fails before their capricious damnation

She is the winepress, they the grapes, her cup runneth over
Drunk on the carnage of her hour in rapturous damnation

Her conquered saints now kneel in worship, drunk on her cruelty
Glad hearts receive her poisoned kiss of venomous damnation

*"Ave, Magna Regina et treminadae majestis!"*

Sister Wisdom cries out her warning before the rising Queen
"Depart from her, partake not of her blasphemous damnation!"

The plea of Wisdom falls on ears deafened by poisoned lips
The mob's cry of "witch!" ignites the pyre of ravenous damnation

Wisdom flickers like a candle, lit by the Queen's hateful torch
A burnt offering to madness of riotous damnation

*"Ave, Magna Regina et treminadae majestis!"*

The Halcyon land that falls to her shall be great nevermore!
A nation crumbles at her scorn to ruinous damnation

Her shadow falls, the dusk has come to an empire's golden age
gods lay slain in the wake of her tenebrous damnation

She tramples them in cruelty, savors freedom's dying screams
Let broken lands resound the hymn of victorious damnation

*"Ave, Magna Regina et treminadae majestis!"*

All hail the savage Queen of Heaven astride the gates of Hell!
Despair on seven hills enthroned, idolatrous damnation

Breathe her wicked name in prayer the grave's embrace receives you!
Sweet savor of death crowned in splendor of gorgeous damnation

Triumph all you Nephilim, exalt her all you Mazikin
Lend thy voice to Cadriel in melodious damnation

*"Ave, Magna Regina et treminadae majestis!"*

# Russell Thorburn

Russell Thorburn is the author of three books of poetry and a recipient of a National Endowment for the Arts Fellowship. The first poet laureate for Michigan's Upper Peninsula, he lives in Marquette with his wife. He spends time each year visiting his eldest son in Los Angeles. Their dual-media exhibit, *Many Names Have Never Been Spoken Here*, interprets the Mojave National Preserve, where they were artists-in-residence. His most recent book of poetry is *Somewhere We'll Leave the World*, published by Wayne State University Press, Made in Michigan Writers Series.

# The Butcher's Song

*The rail bed was frozen with ice*
*In the distance an engine was keeping good time*
-- from Levon Helm singing "A Train Robbery"

All who enter the grocery store
in sloppy boots and ice-crusted brows
lift their voices to us butchers
who cut down into the gristle and bone.
We hold plastic-wrapped pork loins
above your head, and things that matter
slip through our fingers, like satchels
of dollar bills. That express car door open
to the twists in the wind, and some ancient art
of Anaxagoras wants to demonstrate
even the snow must have darkness.

Coffee doesn't matter to me as much
as bourbon a hundred proof that pours through
my own toothy radio in the meat locker.
Something so old bleeds through those words
sung by Levon Helm. Butcher's my name,
the choicest red meat of them all.
Every morning my white coat pocket
bristles with blood from indelible ink pens,
and for the length of a cigarette,
in the break room, it beats heartlessly
with me in a hardbacked chair.

We learn to live with what another
throws away, the packaged red meat
no longer bright, but with rouge
we can make a whole hog carcass dance.
Let that radio back in the meat locker
play its heart out in the cold. Levon
from Arkansas livens up the dead,
in his tribute to Frank and Jesse
James. It is winter here every night,
even if the words disappear into static,
we pause to suck down their meaning.
Boss stalks the aisles for lost money,
a lone dollar bill like a pig's knuckle he says
adds up when you got them all.

197

# Crazy Horse May Have Something to Do with This

We had stripped for the sleeping bag,
always comfortable in the cold
where I'd remember her broad back
and round belly. Smoke, like bits of rope
being untied, rose up through the teepee flaps,
until one of us noticed the flames in the canvas
above us leaping out to the chalked stars
in a winter sky. She bore someone else's child—
the father who owned this farm where we camped,

after a night of wine and piano, his girlfriend
watching us: the extreme cold was where
we could sleep. I was unable to speak to him, spark
words that singed my tongue in love.
I was no Crazy Horse. The teepee juddered aflame.
She was enough, her child, the real father didn't matter.
But the sadness made everything a love song
somehow, like blue-coated men closing on Crazy Horse;

and healing came to us, bracing for the cold
with her baby, running naked from the teepee
to save ourselves; under the skeleton of a moon,
those pointillist stars above shimmering snow—
and we escaped even from these words,
to breathe in ten below for the waiting car,
then sit on frozen seats, hoping the engine
would groan from its stillness;
and we'd grow closer, despite the father

and our own inexperience as parents—
when the starter rattled, we sat in our silence
looking for an answer through an ice-veined
windshield—the teepee aglow—and the engine
finally turned to a man waving his arms
at this two a.m. fire—at us departing with the baby,
not knowing what to feel. Crazy Horse's ghost
shoulder to shoulder with the father.

# Girl with a Broom

I saw the daughter I never had
her head bent at her task,
having learned the art of sweeping
up dirt that comes from not
having a family, her hair dark
as coal parted down the middle
and tied neatly back, sweeping sorrow
without looking up at me,
standing there with my luggage,
a girl bristling compact strokes
to tidy the hotel porch,
and I walked past her, not gawking,
a stranger who happened to love
a woman with the same hair
and able hands, a mother
not there to watch her on her first
job, and couldn't ever forget
our eyes cried out from a life
we had to let go and here
was the daughter we never had,
a broom in her hands
intently strawing.

# Baba Yaga

*Baba Yaga is often seen as evil and scary, but at times, she acts as an aid
to the hero or heroine of the story. Whether she's sweet-tempered or ill-
natured, her wisdom is undisputed; she's as ancient as the dark Russian
forest she occupies and pulls her knowledge from the ages.*

Her house was a Russian fairy tale ready
to walk away on chicken legs.
I couldn't see my hands in the falling snow,
losing more of myself and stepped
on those complaining floorboards
past her sleeping hounds
and wasted time staring at the teeth
of Baba Yaga, a yellow like some piano keys,
her body large as the piano itself,
but able to produce such beautiful notes,
when my hand got lost in their intentions
and wandered through her hair
as if playing a strange music
that ended with my mouth around
her glossy lips, chewed upon
and chapped, as if she was more nervous
than me in her overheated
house built above the deep snow.

She shook loose her long
black hair meant for long hair music,
not for her pupil to suck the eggs
from her yellow teeth—and she screamed,
more animal than human, how
I had disappointed her, fickle
at times, just like her music
from a Russian songbook.
I knew she loved me, though,
despite my ragged cuffs, uncombable
hair under that dirty cap, and she
always invited me to come to her
chicken-legged house clean as any
of those chicken bones her hounds
chewed upon, but how often
her blood-soaked hounds
looked bored with their bones.

Her voice was on hair trigger
and she didn't want to sleep
with a pupil, but as I grabbed
my cap from a chair standing
there in disbelief, with its stiff back
and seat, she changed her mind,
and I wouldn't ever know true music
between two people, if I didn't return
at her bidding, if I didn't seat myself
on that cold bench before her grinning
German piano, her bushel of frizzy hair
burying her eyes, in love with my clumsy
hands trying to figure out the meledy.

# A Reason for Mountains

*It was their quietness that made me lean toward them...*
            --Julio Cortázar

There was a time when the mountains
        could talk, when those rounded shoulders
                belonged to a giant,
                        who slumbered in the green-blond
        scrub that stretched for miles; there was a reason
for mountains in the hatchet heat, to witness a man dying,
                the breath cut off in his esophagus—
                        his hat discarded, water supply gone,
        a dying man on the Mojave Road,
                        if this is what he truly was—a Confederate
wounded at Shiloh, on his way to Colorado,
                who stumbles in sight of the mountains—
        mountains that have forgotten their tongue,
                a dialect of stone that's more than
                        lifeless, sporting vegetal growth.
                Any thinking mountain knows
when to pity you, the evening haze lightening
        in the stubble of stars around its mouth—
                and there is a reason for mountains
                        to be so far away,
        and the time feels like it's less if we stay quietly.

# Appreciation

Thank you to Matt Maki, Claudia Drosen and Janeen Pergrin Rastall for your effort to start the Marquette Poets Circle and to establish the monthly work shop and open mic. Thank you to the Peter White Public Library for hosting the monthly work shop and open mic.

Thank you to all the poets who submitted poems for this anthology. Thank you for your assistance with this publication.

Thank you to Martin Achatz for the preface.

Thank you to Elizabeth J. Bates for the cover photos.

Thank you to Janeen Pergrin Rastall for countless items of help and suggestions during the editing process.

# Index of Titles